Night Flight
to Hanoi

By the Same Author

NIGHT FLIGHT TO HANOI

War Diary
with 11 Poems

by Daniel Berrigan

THE MACMILLAN COMPANY, *New York*
COLLIER-MACMILLAN LTD., *London*

Library of Congress Catalog Card Number: 68-56045

FIRST PRINTING

The Macmillan Company, New York
Collier-Macmillan Canada Ltd., Toronto, Ontario

Printed in the United States of America

ACKNOWLEDGMENTS

The author wishes to acknowledge *The National Catholic Reporter* in which "Letter from Three Jails" originally appeared, *Liberation* in which his poems contained in this book originally appeared, and *Worldview* for his "Mission to Hanoi," Part I and II.

to Philip
another way, toward life

CONTENTS

INTRODUCTION

I met Father Daniel Berrigan for the first time in a Greenwich Village apartment in New York, January 31, 1968, the morning of the day we were to travel together, halfway around the world, to Hanoi. He seemed to me a French worker-priest, with his dark turtleneck shirt, his black trousers, lean body, puckish, wise eyes, cropped hair. Both of us had responded to phone calls from Dave Dellinger, editor of *Liberation* magazine, who had received a telegram from the peace committee of North Vietnam: "In celebration of our New Year Tet holiday, we are preparing to release three captured American pilots to the American peace movement. Please send responsible representative for reception and discussion."

Dave then called Dan Berrigan, who was teaching courses in modern drama and the New Testament (a logical combination, for the likes of him) at Cornell University, and phoned me at Boston University, where I teach political science. One of us, he thought, might be willing to go. Both of us said yes, and so, with a bit of worry about how to pay the travel agency (eventually, for even radicals use the credit system) for two fat airline tickets, Dave decided it would be good if both went—immediately.

We three met the next day in New York, with Tom Hayden, who had made one of the first trips to Hanoi back in 1965, and who had recently been involved in the release of three American prisoners of the National Liberation Front in Cambodia. Meanwhile, the news was traveling fast

about our impending trip; the press reported on the telegram to Dellinger, and two wives of imprisoned fliers flew
into New York from North Carolina to give us letters to
their husbands, as well as letters from other wives of
prisoners. They showed only a slight tension at meeting
objectors to a war their husbands were waging; it helped
perhaps that one of the two emissaries was a Jesuit priest
and the other a professor who had once been an Air Force
bombardier.

The other preflight visit, just before we drove out to
Kennedy Airport, was from a State Department man in
Averell Harriman's office. He offered to validate our passports for travel to North Vietnam, an officially forbidden
destination. Father Berrigan and I had agreed quickly before his arrival that we did not want to recognize the government's right to approve or disapprove travel to any part
of the world, so we politely declined. The State Department
man was concerned over how the fliers would be brought
back to the States; he preferred military transport to civilian
airlines. We agreed to leave it up to the pilots themselves.
This was later to become a point of intense, absurd con-
troversy, argued out with the American ambassador to Laos
in the confines of an old airplane that had just brought all
five of us (Berrigan, me, the three fliers) out of Hanoi.

Father Berrigan and I boarded an SAS flight to Copen-
hagen that Wednesday evening, the first leg of a race to
Vientiane, Laos, hoping to get there in time to catch the
Friday afternoon International Control Commission flight
to Hanoi. For thirty hours we read, ate, talked, changed
planes, tried to sleep: from Copenhagen to Frankfurt to
Rome to Teheran to Karachi to Calcutta to Bangkok to
Vientiane. We arrived in time, only to learn that the Friday
ICC plane had not left Saigon that morning, owing to the
fighting around Tan San Nhut airfield; it was the start of

the NLF Tet offensive. We would have to wait until Tuesday, because the ICC plane flew only six times a month—every Friday and alternate Tuesdays—on a carefully marked-out route, in a carefully timed procedure, so that neither United States bombers nor North Vietnamese gunners would interfere with the flight.

Dan Berrigan and I spent the next sixteen days together: seven days in Laos, seven days in Hanoi, two days en route home. In the following pages, he tells about our time in Hanoi. Our week in Vientiane was a frustrating, fascinating period of waiting; we visited embassies, walked through Buddhist temples, ate with Laotian villagers in their huts, talked to foreign journalists, to a Pathet Lao leader. We heard from young Americans working with the International Volunteer Service who were bitterly critical of the American presence in Vietnam, and also of its aid program in Laos. We walked along the Mekong River, sat on the curb in the sun, were interviewed by American television crews. Finally, the following Friday, just before dusk, we boarded the thirty-year-old, squatting, four-engined Boeing bird, and flew to Hanoi.

In Vientiane and in Hanoi, at mysterious moments before bedtime which I never discovered, Dan Berrigan wrote poems. For two rather silent types, we talked a good deal. He had been raised on a farm in New York State, became a priest and a poet. He visited Africa, studied for two years in Paris, became a radical critic of war and sympathizer with revolutions. At certain moments, the confrontation with conscience was close and painful: a young friend burned himself to death in protest against the war in Vietnam. Sent to Latin America to "cool off," Dan became more radical. There he saw poverty, rebellion, repression: 150,000 human beings burrowed like rats in the dumping grounds of Lima. In the Amazon valley of Brazil, he saw consciousness growing among the peasants ("they were turning from cactus into men") and then the Castello Branco regime rushed in to stifle that growth. Home again, he joined the antiwar march to the Pentagon in 1967, and went to jail.

I liked what Father Berrigan had to say: "When absolutes enter the human scene, we have obsession—and possibly murder." Another time: "If you can't make it on the personal level, then you are abstract, you don't belong—it's not even rational, it's not *embodied*." And: "If God chose to come to earth and join man, this should say something about life, man, woman, flesh." And: "The last thing Christ wanted to do was start a church."

We laughed a lot together during those days. But as I write this now, Dan Berrigan is facing jail for who-knows-how-many-years, because he (and his brother Phil, and others) decided to protest the mass murder of the Vietnam War by destroying draft card files in Baltimore. Of course he violated the law. But he was right. And it is the mark of enlightened citizens in a democracy that they know the difference between law and justice, between what is legal and what is right. It is the mark of wise men to know what is important and what is unimportant. The flesh of Vietnamese men, women, children—the blood of young American soldiers—the anguish of parents grieving over lost children—that is important. The papers and paraphernalia of the system that selects men for war—these are unimportant.

Let us hope that our country will become wise. But until it does—indeed, in order that it should—we as its citizens must act in the wisdom of our own conscience. That, to me, is the ultimate meaning of what Father Daniel Berrigan, in prose and poetry, says and leaves unsaid in the pages that follow.

HOWARD ZINN

PREFACE

It seemed to me, as the war went on and on, that one had to try and operate on two fronts. The war itself had, in a sense, given away the secrets of war; the war had suggested to us, sotto voce, the methods of peace. Those methods went something like this: one war was to be fought on two grounds, Vietnam, and the American ghettos. So it was crucial, in spite of all roadblocks, to be present in both places.

In order to make peace, at least a few Americans had to share, at least in some measure, the life and hard times of Hanoi; the terror, the death from the air. One would have to crouch in a concrete bunker, like a mole with an eagle's microscopic eye gyring overhead. He would have to know death firsthand; the presence of death, the end of rhetoric, the beginning of wisdom.

And in the course of such a war, one had to go to jail. It was an irreplaceable need, a gift not to be refused. You got arrested, were stripped, your body was searched and poked for drugs. You stood in public showers, were issued the denims, were herded about, feared, segregated, counted at odd hours, yelled at.

All to the good. And after all, the scene was no Dachau; you would come out the other side intact, a few pounds lighter, the skin of your soul darkened with insight—the fate of the poor, the Blacks. Knowing white justice for what it is, to the poor; knowing that the D.C. jail is one mortise, one roof and fabric with the D.C. ghetto, a single architecture and intent, the logical "other room" in the haunted house. There were no priest holes any more, you were not riding circuit in tony Elizabethan England, hiding out, moving on. No; you were American to the bone, though you had your own convictions about American adventuring—pacification-cum-napalm, racism-cum-Bible, the church-going military and the militant churchmen.

Man, you'd better save your soul, no one else could do it for you now, it was midnight at the Pentagon, late as literal hell. Move when told, or sit there on your hunkers and take what would come; the vans were rolling up, the lights were on, fierce as bared teeth, the exterminator had turned about, there was a tiger in your flank.

The teeth hurt, but the hurt was superficial. The tiger bit mortally elsewhere. After all, you were white and middling, *sacerdos in aeternum*, it wouldn't do to make overkill here and now. Besides, the ring of soldiers was uncertain, they had been marched out of the military temple on a dirty errand; they weren't mercenaries, this was a new scene. It wasn't Hanoi, not by a long shot.

Hanoi! At home the jail was joined to the ghetto; more, the American ghetto and the Hanoi "operation" were a single enterprise. Both were conceived by military minds, in essence; pararacist and plenary, total, a total war, war in both cases, in both places. A racist cleanup, a segregation triumph, a zoo under fire, a condemned playground for the war game, an ordinance proving ground.

Proving—what? Why, that we're the great, the pure, the best, the unique and chosen, deciders and destructors. We separated, by divine right, wheat from chaff, gooks from whites, the living from the dead.

I thought, in both places, of unity, community, communication. The old, good words, bathed in a fresh light. Man was a unity; we were not a nation of county coroners, the world was not to be a morgue, we had no right to dismember the living, to read our future in their bared guts. Community; put men together! The military nation state was not a community; it was a walking zombie, stitched together out of obscene rags and tags, a rifle for a backbone, sawdust for a heart, a cadaver programmed to the jargon of realpolitik, a horror stalking by night, flapping the skies, dropping hot faeces in the eyes of sleeping children. No. Say no. Communicate. Get to Hanoi, the action was there, you had to see it, to tell it like it was.

Hanoi; that ancient eastern icon decked out in French robes, the artist's stroke lingering along eye and hand, long and contemplative, the lotus in the fingers. We were there toward the end of January, we got in by the skin of our teeth, while the hottest horror of three years blazed away to the south. The Vietnamese were celebrating the Tet holiday, with a new twist. We were Guy Fawkes, and the scarecrow, and the hidden and sought; they tricked and we retreated.

In the peace movement, you got used to being without power; that was your name. Then the invitation from Hanoi—and suddenly, what power! Zinn and I grinned at one another across three continents, like carved pumpkins lit in the night. Why, we were doing what all the king's armies and all the king's men couldn't do. We were going where Mr. Rusk couldn't go, or Bundy, or the President himself.

D.C. jail, North Vietnam. Mobility, inwardness; tumult, travel; incarceration, incineration. Take it, eat it up. You couldn't die where you'd been born. The earth was shedding its skin with every new season, it was pulling out from under you like a rug. You had to keep running to keep living, a moving target had more chance. Or, you had to go under, to hibernate, to live like a dreaming animal, off the fat and marrow of your mind. To say, here, there and everywhere, like Mrs. Rooney; Christ, what a planet!

Every book that deals, as this one tries to, with the news about today, finds itself fairly buried before it is born. Last week's omelette. This week is still in the egg shells. I sit here, breaking eggs to make an Easter, to feed the living as I hope, good news for bad. Some ten or twelve of us (the number is still uncertain) will, if all goes well (ill?) take our religious bodies during this week to a draft center in or near Baltimore. There we shall, of purpose and fore-thought, remove the A-1 files, sprinkle them in the public street with homemade napalm and set them afire. For which act we shall, beyond doubt, be placed behind bars for some portion of our natural lives, in consequence of our inability to live and die content in the plagued city, to say peace peace when there is no peace, to keep the poor poor, the homeless homeless, the thirsty and hungry thirsty and hungry.

Our apologies, good friends, for the fracture of good order, the burning of paper instead of children, the anger-ing of the orderlies in the front parlor of the charnel house. We could not, so help us God, do otherwise. For we are sick at heart, our hearts give us no rest for thinking of the Land of Burning Children. And for thinking of that other Child, of whom the poet Luke speaks. The infant was taken up in the arms of an old man, whose tongue grew resonant and vatic at the touch of that beauty. And the old man spoke; this child is set for the fall and rise of many in Israel, a sign that is spoken against.

Small consolation; a child born to make trouble, and to die for it, the first Jew (not the last) to be subject of a "definitive solution." He sets up the cross and dies on it; in the Rose Garden of the executive mansion, on the D.C. Mall, in the courtyard of the Pentagon. We see the sign, we read the direction; you must bear with us, for His sake. Or if you will not, the consequences are our own.

For it will be easy, after all, to discredit us. Our record is bad; troublemakers in church and state, a priest married despite his vows, two convicted felons. We have jail records, we have been turbulent, uncharitable, we have failed in love for the brethren, have yielded to fear and despair and pride, often in our lives. Forgive us.

We are no more, when the truth is told, than ignorant beset men, jockeying against all chance, at the hour of death, for a place at the right hand of the dying One.

We act against the law at a time of the Poor Peoples' March, at a time, moreover, when the government is announcing ever more massive paramilitary means to confront disorder in the cities. It is announced that a computerized center is being built in the Pentagon at a cost of some seven million dollars, to offer instant response to outbreaks anywhere in the land; that, moreover, the government takes so serious a view of civil disorder that federal troops with war experience in Vietnam will have first responsibility to quell civil disorder.

The implications of all this must strike horror in the mind of any thinking man. The war in Vietnam is more and more literally being brought home to us. Its inmost meaning strikes the American ghettos: one war, one crime against the poor, waged (largely) by the poor, in servitude to the affluent. We resist and protest this crime.

Finally, we stretch out our hands to our brothers

throughout the world. We who are priests, to our fellow priests. All of us who act against the law, turn to the poor of the world, to the Vietnamese, to the victims, to the soldiers who kill and die; for the wrong reasons, for no reason at all, because they were so ordered—by the authorities of that public order which is in effect a massive institutionalized disorder.

We say killing is disorder; life and gentleness and community and unselfishness is the only order we recognize. For the sake of that order, we risk our liberty, our good name. The time is past when good men can remain silent, when obedience can segregate men from public risk, when the poor can die without defense.

We ask our fellow Christians to consider in their hearts a question that has tortured us, night and day, since the war began. How many must die before our voices are heard, how many must be tortured, dislocated, starved, maddened? How long must the world's resources be raped in the service of legalized murder? When, at what point, will you say no to this war?

We have chosen to say, with the gift of our liberty, if necessary of our lives, the violence stops here, the death stops here, the suppression of the truth stops here, the war stops here.

We wish also to place in question by this act all suppositions about normal times, longings for an untroubled life in a somnolent church, that neat timetable of ecclesiastical renewal which, in respect to the needs of men, amounts to another form of time serving.

Redeem the times! The times are inexpressibly evil. Christians pay conscious—indeed religious—tribute to Caesar and Mars; by approval of overkill tactics, by brinkmanship, by nuclear liturgies, by racism, by support of genocide. They embrace their society with all their heart, and abandon the cross. They pay lip service to Christ and military service to the powers of death.

And yet, and yet, the times are inexhaustibly good, solaced by the courage and hope of many. The truth rules, Christ is not forsaken. In a time of death, some men—the resisters, those who work hardily for social change, those who preach and embrace the unpalatable truth—such men overcome death, their lives are bathed in the light of the resurrection, the truth has set them free. In the jaws of death, of contumely, of good and ill report, they proclaim their love of the brethren.

We think of such men, in the world, in our nation, in the churches; and the stone in our breast is dissolved; we take heart once more.

DANIEL BERRIGAN, S.J.

LETTER FROM THREE JAILS

A Clash of Absurdities

At midnight on October 22, Daniel Berrigan, S.J., was ar-rested at the Pentagon for his participation in an anti-Vietnam protest demonstration. He was charged with a misdemeanor for "refusing to move on when told." On Tuesday, October 24, he was offered bail but refused "in order to continue fasting and see what would happen." He fasted six days. On Friday, October 27, he was persuaded to accept bail; on the street he heard a radio report of the arrest of his brother, Father Philip Berrigan, a Josephite priest in Baltimore, for an anti-draft demonstration.

In the accompanying "jail notes" he describes his im-prisonment, about which he says this is "an astoundingly joyful time and from the point of view of Christians a chance to write our own 'Acts.' Remember—'Grave trou-bles continue, but a great door has opened.' "

The strangeness and inner difficulty at coming to terms with the new life thrust on one here.

Last night, a lurid "confrontation," which seems more and more to me like the collision of two absurdities. One of them plate-armored like a clanking dinosaur. The other the improvidence and absurdity of those who put their trust in "spirit and power."

Thousands of soldiers, air-lifted from distant points—an inconvenience that ensured their truculence in facing the "job": ourselves.

So we are living out today in a nauseous green chicken house. Each of us has the run of the place, and the lights are on all night, something again to do with chickens. On

3

the farm, we used to give them twenty-four hour light to keep them working hard. Here, it is rather a matter of making the atmosphere nervy, of keeping us on edge. Like the rule that says we never walk out of doors, so that we can see only a patch of sky at the upper branches of a tree.

The courage required of the girls and older people last night as they sat before the exterminator and his AM tracks, grinding to a reluctant halt at the very edge of their bodies. Contrary to official hopes, it helped us see how the battle line extends bloodily across our own lives.

A good joke; we had come to D.C. to fast and to hold workshops in protest. Now the Cornell contingent is totally scattered in the grab-bag of these hours—some in jail, some fasting here, some back in Ithaca.

What a time, when theology is written on the run, in snatches and fits and starts. And yet I can say with all my heart's approval, we have come full circle and are back in the prison of Antiochus or Herod, speaking through the bars.

Last night's "nerve gas" was not sprayed at us from cans. But it came through the air, nonetheless; the big voice from the façade, announcing again and again into the darkness what would happen to those who didn't take the option and get out. It came through. And it stung. It has come to this, during this war, that the government is acting at home and abroad in a perfectly consistent way. On both fronts, American power is the active, virulent enemy of human hope.

Now, I wish it were possible to give the flavor of the community here. Everyone is doing his own "thing." Resisters of all kinds and degrees. An ex-Green Beret is fasting even from water. He speaks lucidly and logically, but I fear much for such a step. What will happen to him when the guards find out, as they certainly will? What will happen to his superb health? He has gone the full journey from specialized murder to pacifism and vegetarianism.

Five hours last night at the cold proscenium of a Greek stage: the Pentagon, the lights, the stern tragic chorus of troops, the protagonists, the iron *anagke* of the White House, reaching even as far as our domestic distant lives, brought suddenly near at a point of mortal crisis.

So now I am forty-six, and at length in jail, and two reflections occur:

1. Why was I so long retarded from so crucially formative a happening?

2. What's the big joke, You there?

Today, things were not altogether easy; one feels pain and joy together in the same guts. When we were locked up last night, it seemed to me that we had been let, for some brief time, out of the horror and willful idiocy of the world into a place where goodness gathers by privilege, after long loneliness and struggle. Who is free anyway, and who is unfree, given the world—given the Church?

I wish it were possible to write a poem. Everything, from the radiators, four-toned with rust, to the tympanum of the old heating valves, to the aggressive chaplain, to the phalanx of helmets and stern non-faces last night—everything so exceeds the prosaic that I am quite at a loss.

On the radio a senator denounces the Pentagon demonstrators; 99.99 percent of the American people, he pontificates, can never agree with such activity. And the President declares he will see the war through, in spite of such as us. It has not penetrated official consciousness that the Pentagon is itself the enemy. And who will remove or levitate, or exorcise that one?

It seems to me a kind of tribute to us, paid by the expectation of a violent people, that the smallest failures in non-violent conduct raise a storm. While the war goes on, the war protesters are subjected to another set of rules entirely. It is, however, entirely correct that we be so judged. It is in accord with our moral claim about the superiority of spirit over force. And even when I take the word of eyewitnesses about the clashes on Saturday night, a good deal that is reprehensible remains from the point of view of the ideal we had declared.

Transferred today from dormitories to cells, for various crimes; mine being the refusal to pay the fine. So here I am with about thirty others, the hard core resisters, fasters, limp-goers, etc. This is going to be the simplest sort of house work I have ever had—a john in the corner, a sink and a bed. Some light gets through the barred window. It is a narrower ambience than the gorges and skies of Cornell.

The court, quickly set up this morning to dispose of all the remaining cases, had the stale air of a kangaroo pouch. The presiding judge, quickly sworn in, was ill at ease before the hirsute, curious, intent faces. He seemed determined to conquer his greenness by administering the sternest and purest form of justice. So my punishment was the double of the man who appeared immediately before me, judged guilty of the same misdemeanor. I will evidently have some quiet hours ahead to figure this one out.

There is a great shouting at one another and cheering for one another, as some limp-goers are dragged in. Several are on water fasts. Many have refused to go before judges. There seem to be many styles of saying "no." Meantime, the chaplain addresses me soberly through the bars; he is quaffing a can of orange juice as he speaks. I think he would like to administer a Catholic loyalty oath. But it doesn't quite go over. A hard face, a hard manner. I suspect he has me catalogued for a heretic.

October 24. The third jail in three days. Now the D.C. jail. Arrived at 4:30 P.M. to face the humiliating public stripping and search for dope, etc. All were in good spirits. For the first time, I put on the prison blue jeans and denim shirt; a clerical attire I highly recommend for a new church.

Six and one-half hours later we were still without supper. Some twenty of us with twenty of the prisoners who had returned from work crews, were locked in a forty-by-twenty-foot cage. Meantime, an unexplained "count" went on. One prisoner collapsed, vomiting on the floor, the temperature mounted. It was one of the few times that I knew fear. Perhaps I had bitten off too much "reality." But I made it after all.

We got in to supper about midnight, segregated from the others, having passed in the corridor the cheerful group of our brothers who had refused to cooperate since we left Virginia. In their midst was a young fellow who was almost entirely unconscious and who had been for many hours without medical attention. They were crying for help, and I was determined to get to the chaplain who (as we learned later) finally got medical aid about 1 or 2 A.M.

We were segregated from the others for the first meal by a rather brutal guard. I took a half cup of coffee and a little milk and plenty of sugar in tribute to my ulcer.

"In framing an ideal, we may assume what we wish. But we should avoid impossibilities." (Aristotle)

The ideal here is manifestly a modest one, but presupposes reserves of good humor, balance of mind, and inner freedom—a modest utopia in fact. I hope my Order can come to understand the workable limits of what I am trying to do. Perhaps through this and similar action a few of the younger men might be impelled to get with human history in a more personal and imaginative way. What I do is certainly not done from obsession or a mental straitjacket; jail and fasting are by now well-worn tools of human change.

Time and again it is a source of rejoicing for me when the prisoners discover who I am. A fruitful discussion invariably follows. I have a strong impression that places like this are the most logical ones for human beings to open their hearts to one another. Here, values are hemmed in by public oppression, but communities coalesce in the fires of social protest, their hands warmed by a passion for human justice. How neutral and enervated appear the usual groupings of Sunday worshipers in comparison! The point here is not moral judgment, but simply to recall to myself that the Church is invited to be where the action is.

Toward 5 A.M. seven or eight more protestors were pushed in with us. They were part of a group arrested at an induction center in D.C. yesterday. As we have our community under way, they are not coming to a vacuum.

I keep thinking and praying as best I can, for the seven

non-cooperators who are locked somewhere in the build-ing, perhaps in the same corridor where we passed them last night. No food, some of them have not taken water in days, they are undoubtedly without a mattress on the floor.

Some are ill from a combination of cold, monotony and neglect. Things developed so quickly. It seems as though I have lived many months since last Sunday.

Last night toward 1 A.M. I proposed a kind of Friends' Meeting. We gathered in a circle on the floor in silence for about an hour, alternated in those healing rhythms that take one gently into a better perspective and a clearer air. We held hands for a moment's silence at the end, and so to bed and what passed for sleep.

The day does not seem so long when there are a few books. I think of how, at home, I take my big loaded shelves for granted, and have the luxury of picking and choosing in a way that seems almost obscene from here. Like a voracious *Hausfrau* at a supermarket.

I have not thought a great deal about the war. Strangely enough it seems that one comes to a center, by way of the war, whose fiery outer reaches protect the heart of the matter—community, the omnipresent possibility of love, waiting like an abandoned child for the moment of recog-nition.

"Why should you be stricken any more? You will revolt more and more. The whole head is sick and the whole heart faint" (Is. 1:5). "Except the Lord of Hosts had left to us a very small remnant, we would have been as Sodom, we would have been as Gemorrah" (I:9)

One of the least bearable of sights is the injury of the helpless, whether on the line Saturday when the paratroopers used rifle clubs to beat the linked arms of the protesters, or here, the sight of bodies being more or less deliberately struck against corners, walls, or dropped to the concrete floor when the prisoners are pulled or borne from place to place, refusing, as some of them do, to walk. At such a moment one knows both the gravity and the grace of flesh. What saves even worse things from happening is the continuous talk that goes up from the other prisoners, exhorting the guards to mercy, relieving the exasperation that attends on their hated burdens.

It is not so much that political solutions fall short of effecting social change. It is nearer the point to say that today politics itself is corrupted in its deepest intention. A chasm has opened between the meaning of the common good as public fact and spiritual change as a personal postulate. But to be a political man implies openness to conversion of heart. The rest is vanity.

The obscenity of "scientific objectivity" applied to areas of feeling, like a throttling hand at a throat.

"*Attention! Attention!*" A quasi-military yell, based on the most inhuman assumptions about others, is also—strangely—a summons to freedom. Attention! Concentration! Intensity!

The sun comes up from afar, like a bearer of good news weary of his own burden. He arrives faint, with hardly the life left to breathe life into men. But he transfigures the faces, for a few moments. The young prisoners are at the barred door talking softly to the guards. The protesters have no objection, literally not one, to conditions here. So they make peace in the unlikeliest places. The guards come to stare and glower, and stay to talk. Sometimes. Too much success would dull the fine edge of danger and chance.

One of the guards just said he wouldn't be surprised if we were "toted back to Occaquan today." Certainly a great deal of the treatment we have seen can only be put down to crude spite.

Like a primitive potlatch for the makings of a marvelous Halloween bonfire. Everyone puts his tobacco and papers into the middle of the floor. So a natural circle forms periodically. No one smokes alone or hoards anything.

The younger prisoners are not baffled, nor is their fervor dampened by the monotony of the prison. This, even though the regime is designed to produce a high yield of human vegetables.

There is news, and most of it bad, from the Hole. There, seven of our brothers spent the night naked on concrete, in near freezing cold, stretched next to an open non-flushing privy. At one point the guards attached wrist clamps to them, tightened them unbearably and dragged the men naked across the floors. They have no food or drink. Thus far the Great Society.

The only absolutes at work here are the extreme variables of love, in its sinuous, subtle, always exciting movement. One of the men does this, another does that, another a third thing. Each spins like a spider out of his guts, his own lifeline. Result: a trembling daring web of great precision and strength—which we can all walk.

No need of organizing among us. Each acts so spontaneously and truthfully, out of the heart and experience and the flesh, the concurrence on essentials is inevitable and right.

Variety! A two-edged sword. I think of how many in this

room have the long-distance patience of Lincoln, the impassioned urgency of eighteenth-century nation-makers. And they are in jail; a commentary on a society that cannot bear with its own patriots. Springs in the desert, flowers in the barrels of rifles, life in the smoking breach of death.

Am I really here? I will be asking myself in a few days—was I ever here?

The fooling with which the young are skilled in urging time by. A group has rolled a cigarette the size of a small votive candle. They are passing it around like a peace pipe. The atmosphere makes all sorts of madness logical. These young fellows clown like adolescents. But last night some of them faced the guards' violence and beatings with a calm that would have done honor to Gandhi.

One of the young prisoners comes at me like a red guard. He is puzzled, annoyed, bitched up. "You're a believer, but you're a good man. Why do you need Jesus? Create your own gods!"

To him, I drag along a series of tin cans, empty and noisy, the historical debris and waste of religion: inert ideas; war-making cardinals; the hot, anti-human, anti-history, pure, puritan, alienated "religious" community. My difficulty with him is not that I don't see his point. God knows I have struggled with it for years. But he is as intolerant as a barracuda, and won't admit of any good in a mixed scene. In spite of it all, what is the story of man, or of religion, except a despised remnant, struggling in the toils of violence tightened by the world and by the world's religions? But on the other hand, where did God ever announce himself as a majoritarian anyway? The big text on consensus from Isaias is, as one might have predicted, a corruption of the original.

Long discussions are provoked by the presence of men in the Hole. Yesterday three of them gave up and came back to us. Also to be dealt with are the immaturity of many, the settling pall of a routine. When is resistance a mature response to the systems and powers that claim our lives? And when does it become a petulant form of egoism? A hard line to draw—let alone hew to.

Segregation: We're locked all day in the dorm. The regular prisoners, about 95 percent of them black, are supposed to have no contact with us. Reasons officially given vary; the threat of sexual assault, threats against our political ideas. (The excuses are aired often; it must be because they smell bad.)

Only once in a while is it admitted openly that officials have enough trouble trying to deal with the Black Muslims, who are canny and determined, and if pushed would tie the place in a knot.

Well, except for a few of us, most of whom are in the Hole, any resemblance to Black Muslim know-how is purely coincidental. This in fact was demonstrated on Saturday at the Pentagon; we are a tempestuous crew, very mixed, thoughtful and thoughtless.

Like a Maine shoreline after a drowning tide, the personalities slowly surface, dry, stand. The moody, the immature, the contemplative. Those whose lives prepare them for this, those who were unready, and so are threatened with destruction.

This A.M. three guards, to make a point, ordered everyone to his feet for the count. What point! To show the

S.O.B.'s who's in charge here. Four or five would not get off the floor; they are to be dragged off to the Hole. We'll see.

It looms over us, but not so deep or so wide as to drown us.

Today the guards seized one young fellow, twisted his arm, tore his clothing, dragged him across the floor, yelling that he was bound for the Hole. When three guards returned with a sergeant, they dealt with the rest of us, berating us for "unmanly disruption." At this point no one of us would stand. So he took the count in a fury. We sat where we were. Five minutes later our friend returned to us in a fresh shirt and a big grin.

This far the A.M.

There is still no satisfaction in the case of our companions who remain in the Hole. They have refused clothing, food and water. For at least two of them it is now the sixth day of their water fast.

There are sixteen of us at present count; several were released today.

Visitors—Tom Quigley and Father McKenna from the local Jesuit church.

I wish it were possible to think noble thoughts or to write big words, or to have a sense of holiness or wholeness. But my pencil is dryer than my mouth. What keeps me going is the sense, however obscure, of communion with the victims, and the immediate presence of my friends here.

Friday. This is the day of Phil's action in Baltimore. (*Oremus pro fratribus in periculo.*)

"Give honor to the Lord of Hosts, to him only. Let him be your fear, and let him be your dread" (Is. 8:13).

I thought of how this characterizes my friends here. Of

course, there is a fine electrified line between fear as a
death dealer and fear as another human emotion, to be
dealt with, walked with, as a man walks with his shadow
or his sex or his catarrh. But walks.

Last night another Quaker meeting with long periods of
silence. Then a discussion, the threads of which go into
deeper meanings of these days; the community of poor
around the world, religion, and especially Catholicism. A
rather general and generally thoughtful critique of the
Church. A new style of belief, apparent in a different but
analogous way, among students, too. The common note
being—why keep alive something that has stiffened and
hardened beyond all serviceability? Is there a point at
which one withdraws the tubes and bottles and expensive
intensive care from the dying? Where would one go who
wished today to enter a mendicant order? General interest
in the little brothers and sisters of Jesus.

I note in these young activists:

Interiority. They move skillfully and naturally through
their own guts and heart. Honesty toward a corrupt and
violent society makes for honesty with themselves. The air
in lungs as pure as the outer air. They swim freely and
totally in the here and now, like the mynah bird in Hux-
ley's novel. The rhythm of days, so monotonous and enervating to monotonous men, thus comes to a pitch of excite-
ment and surprise that charges everything.

O Great Society, to what shall I compare thee? Shall the
symbol of these days be our communal toothbrush or the
beds sans sheets or the open-style johns or the affluent
guards or the sun streaming like a stroke frm Degas' brush,
the great eye upon the blind, seeing us who cannot see
him?

Intelligence. They are well read, they are capable of discipline as they are incapable of being pushed about. Dangerous, as a good mind is a danger to the mindless. A fine sword, a refusal to wound. They should be in public office, in the kingdom of the meek, the boroughs of the strong. They should be the Supreme Court and the Senate. *(News report: Senator Fulbright made his analysis to an almost empty house. Toward the end, a few senators drifted in. They had been listening to the World Series. Rome burned brightly.)* They should be in the White House. *(Item: The President sharply chided the protesters, acclaimed the soldiers, assured the nation that we would continue our commitment, would ride our tiger, would bring home the coonskin.)*

They should be Pope. With the College of Cardinals composed of, say, the Beatles, Malcolm X (posthumously), Debray (on condition of nonviolence), Robert Lowell, Tom Merton (who would smile and refuse), Corita (to issue flowered press releases), two members of the *Phoenix* crew, an astronaut each from Russia and the U.S.A., Marianne Moore and one Brooklyn left fielder designated by her.

The sun makes it; brilliant, conspiratorial, unfrenzied, uncozened, uncribbed, unbusted. We might make it.

Hereupon, a poem.

Big Bro Sun who sprung you that you sprout from the
    Heinz can,
    a big racing vine, a hobo miracle?
I turned my back to meet, in camera, the black revolution-
    aries
    of my heart and lo you touched the door with a fist light
      as

catspaw; Jesus! I'm here.
If I fade down the street after some three-balled usurious
    hock
    man death; oh you stand there giving away all my sec-
      ond hands,
    left feet, eyeballs, blood banks, marrow, narrow squeaks,
      soup
    bones. Be then a 16 hr. day, time-and-a-half for saving
      day-
    light. Stand there. Shout it loud. Give it away. I'll pay.
    I'll be
Back, tell them.

Friday morning. The big shots, lawyers, cigar-bearing floradoras and fawners come in. If we'd known you were coming, we'd have mixed a cake (in the toilet bowl) and baked it by successive incubation (one hour per sitter).

They snooped into and peered down the flushing ex-crapolators, looking for their lost faces. We sat around chanting, hands off the gold fish!

Resolution. Tonight I will take in the cat, read Psalm 21, wash three socks, win at poker. I will then memorize, backward and forward fifty times, the exit sign above the barred door. For exercise, I will hang from the clock hands. Finally I will cleanse my conscience and lay me down on a bezor stone. Thank you, Ben Franklin.

NIGHT
FLIGHT
TO
HANOI

Prayer

I left Cornell
with half a wit; six mismated socks
ski underwear, a toothbrush,
passport, one hundred good
green dollars, their faces
virtuous as ancestors,
the chamois sack
Karl Meyer gave me years ago, handmade
by dispossessed Georgia Negroes.

Later, dismay; no Testament.
I must construct, out of oddments, abrasions,
vapor trails, dust, petty cabs,
three crosshatch continents, Brooks Brothers embassies,
their male models dressed to kill—

all He meant and means. I touch
shrapnel and flesh, and risk my reason
for the truth's sake, an ignorant hung head.

Man of one book, stand me in stead.

Hanoi, The Patient Revolution

I am setting this down on February 26, as the reverberations of our trip to Hanoi recede. I also wish to pay ironic tribute to the visit of a State Department official who arrived here this afternoon and treated me to an hour and a half of small talk and double-talk. He is so young, and so completely cut to the bureaucratic cloth; I found him excelling beyond praise in the old game of which Socrates spoke. That is to say, he is skilled at making the worse cause appear the better. And to that degree, he is probably on the rise within his department. The difficulty is (and of course the point is a picayune one) that across the world he and his fraternity represent a mortal danger for the survival of man. The armory of Machiavellian politesse!

He was able to assure me with the utmost conviction (and that steady gaze, which has its origin in the Tom Swift novel) that (1) I had nothing "new or interesting" to bring from Hanoi, and that (2) I could have exerted a "powerful and primary influence" upon the North Vietnamese if only I had been able to convey the American urgency that the killing should stop.

Now these are indeed noble sentiments, and one must make serious note of them. The difficulty is, of course, that they are expressed in an atmosphere of absolute war supremacy and conscienceless application of technology. But my real difficulty goes deeper than this. It has simply to do with the fact that I have seen the victims. And this sight of the mutilated dead has exerted such inward change upon me that the words of corrupt diplomacy appear to me more and more in their true light. That is to say—as words spoken in enmity against reality. And that, of course, is a very old and carefully specified sin, especially in the biblical tradition.

I must insist upon a contrast; indeed the contrast between the fact of Hanoi and the words of Washington is very nearly the only weaponry that the American peace movement can claim. And it does little good, in the task of getting at the truth, to claim that the peace movement is interested only in those black and white contrasts set up by a prevenient conscience, which has immunized itself against the coarse "facts of life." The point is, I would think, that those in the movement who rate highest in intelligence, candor, and passion for truth have been exposed not to the fictions of black and white, but to the facts of life and death. A very different matter indeed.

I could, at the risk of personal cruelty, make large capital out of the exchange with my friend this evening. But apart from cruelty, the reflections would lead us far from the point. *Pace* the State Department, the world is moving massively in another direction than that dictated by the small band of respectable men in Washington who have, for some time now, legitimated murder and expanded murder into genocide. The truth is that their rhetoric leaves one cold—with the cold of death itself. Their language is increasingly narcissistic—it persuades no one but themselves. And even in the process of self-persuasion one sees that flickering of the eye and turning aside from the inquiring gaze, the alienation from an acceptance of truth that is a form of acceptance of self. But the powers and dominations of Washington have no power over me; moreover, they are increasingly losing their power over American lives.

The nation is spinning in the most profound spiritual turmoil in its history. A little, broken, unbreakable Asian nation is working an enormous change in the spiritual constitution of the Western giant. O Altitudo! the meek shall inherit the earth; or at least that portion of the earth which destiny and bloodletting and an unkillable sense of history and the rightness of cosmic ecology have allotted to them.

(I am going to try as carefully as I can in what follows to consult the rather hectic and desultory notes taken in the process of our trip. I shall be most attentive to my literal notes when they refer to important exchanges with interesting men. In the broader issues and larger meetings and experiences I shall rely upon a combination of the text before me and my own reflections.)

Vientiane

We are on the eve of what promises to be our departure
on the last, impossible flight of our voyage. Into the North!
Like that single inch which completes a seven-league leap.
Can it be true that, in going to face the prisoners of war,
Zinn and I are truly leading them out of prison? Or are we
not bringing them from prison back to a prison society?
Are we indeed men who can truly free others? And are the
fliers men who are capable of becoming free men?

Or are we doing something entirely different? Are we
leading children by the hand from one prison into a larger
prison yard? What account will they have to give of themselves? And if they have become free men in prison, what
alternative would be truly open to them except to desert,
to condemn the war, and to reject once and for all the
slavery that hems them in?

It has struck me; we are going on a mission, beyond the
freeing of three men, to free or to invite into freedom our
own society. It occurs to me beyond any doubt that Americans are "prisoners of war," locked in dungeons of illusion,
of fear, of hatred and contempt and joylessness; all of us
hearing the closure in our faces of the hinge of fate,
strangers to our own history, to moral passion, to the
neighbor, strangers to the immense and vagrant and splen-
did mysteries of life itself, the forms of community that
await the "trial of peace," men who advocate formal and
legalized murder as a method of social change. But how
will new men be born, except they will to be born?

Vientiane, and *Ecce!* the troubled duet enters. Troubled
because the same system that lays the wall-to-wall carpet

and installs the air-conditioner in the ambassy office here and welcomes us in a civilized way—that system rains horror and death on the innocent some three hundred miles away. Such reflections must occur; they save us once and for all from captivation by pure motives. The truth is that Zinn and I are tolerated by the powerful because we hold their myths captive by the short hairs. Only the despised peace people, the dubious Americans, the vilified and imprisoned, can save the fliers.

Indeed, once we push beyond the borders of our country it becomes clear that power is powerless, that all the king's army and all the king's men cannot accomplish what we are setting out to do. So our powerlessness is, at least for a time, a source of immense power—with the government and with the "enemy." But tread carefully!

Several meetings already between ourselves and newsmen. The difference between "newsmen" and "new men" is perhaps more than verbal. The first struck me as stuffed like sacks with old newsprint, with yesterday's stale lies. ("But don't you think North Vietnam should also stop the war?") The second, Ah! he is not yet born. But I know his face by heart.

Peace as balance of terror, "Realpolitik," brinkmanship, hot lines and cold war—the lies, the lies explode in the face of the helpless and the poor. Which is the greater outrage—that the innocent die under the bombs, or that the poor are enlisted to launch the bombers? What more incredible disruption of the right order of nature than this; that killers and victims, on orders from the white power elite, should show each other the faces of the African slave and the Asian colonial!

The biography of the white Westerner. He requires (1) someone to kill for him and (2) someone to die for him.

His power is such that he can arrange both requirements, that of vicarious executioner and of vicarious corpse.

The Chanceries and Pentagons can concoct a rhetoric to justify their murders. But one thing they can never do. And this is our hope and the one thing which we count as crucial. They cannot create guerrillas. Which is to say, they cannot create and sustain relationships to other men, and to the land.

Howard and I like to sit on the curb in front of the hotel, like two peasants, letting the unkillable flow of life—paddy cabs, scooters, wanderers, cyclists, truckers, shoppers—well and flow over and through us, and wash clean the stables of our impure hope, our fainthearted thought of tomorrow, our stale tags of fear, ennui, our ambiguous "movements," our inability to "connect," to fold inward, to *be*, finally! Sitting there blinking in the benign sun of dusk, we experience a paradigm of all that immense human variety, that huge delicate beating fan, those hearts, all the hue and cry of existence. What is it that you most fear? It is life itself.

In the guarded playground the real world flows around like the calliope figures around the filthy turbulent machinery at the center.

In embassy after embassy Zinn and I see what "foreign service" does to human faces. Dead souls. They fix their gaze on middle distance and announce the utter impossibility of all suggestions, breakthroughs, alternatives, nuances, of all options in fact that have not already occurred to them. Among such men we have met with only one exception; his personal unhappiness is apparent in his inability to compose that mortician triumph, the chancery countenance. He knows sorrow and joy. He will not thrive.

The Thailand Embassy. The East learns from the West

the stale tricks, the delaying tactics, the shuffling of paper, which are the songs of life gone stale. The scuffed, unpainted desk glowers. The furniture exudes a sullen furtive threat. A chair says, Sit on me friend, I will yet ride you.

A visit to a notable. The main street was clogged with crowds in front of the peeling villa of the prince. A bear cub of the young princess was on the loose, and the news had gotten about. The great fear was for the proper diet for the animal, if too long exposed to bananas and papaya, at the hands of the populace.

Beyond frivolity, the plaza sputters and buzzes, like live wires fallen in a storm; danger, rumor, coup and counter-coup. The city is like a top-heavy imperial elephant; too many diplomats, too much complication, intrigue, too little common sense.

The old purgatorial myths of detention, purification and joyous release. Here we sit by the waters of the Mekong. But how shall we sing the songs of Israel in a strange land? Awaiting the airplane, awaiting the prisoners, awaiting ourselves. Like Kafka shadows, waiting for their counterparts. How can we become ourselves, except we undergo that final journey, its passage granted to us by the enemy, its provisions cut to the bone?

Waiting: Vientiane

The birds of dawn are crying, drawing
   the great sun into conflict
   a contested light

the bloody challenge taken, the spurred leap,
       roof after roof.
   Visualize such a bird
  as you imagine the sun
     a black carapace
    a fruit bitter as limes
       a bull studded with flags
a guerrilla striking while the iron is hot.

    Sun
   who alone cocks eye (eyeing that cock)
      and not
    burns his socket blind; from his
intolerable equinox, seeing in the sea
     himself rampant, eye to eye
  lives in that cry nor turns to stone
      nor no, shall die.

A solid week of waiting. It is Friday, and in a few hours
we will know our fate—whether or not the plane will land.
If it does not come we must return to Cambodia and seek a
plane into Hanoi through Mainland China. As yet, neither
of us can face returning to the United States without a
substantial effort at getting the mission done, and the fliers
out.

Meantime our thoughts are increasingly sober. The mission is calculated to outrage some on both sides. There will be activists, dry as bones and incapable of compassion, who will score us for selling out to the military. Then, some of the hawks, whose eye and claw are sharpened mightily these days, will descend upon us for not going into Hanoi with our passports honor bright. But I say, a plague alike on peregrine and pigeon. We shall harken to our own drummer.

And I think tonight of all those I love, so far removed, those whom the sun now visits strongly and coldly, a wintry day no doubt. Those for whose love I must "love honor more." My mother and father, gently and silently cresting yet another redoubtable wave in an old age that refuses them peace. Philip and his friends awaiting trial in the same cause as mine. Jim and Rosalie, Tom and Honor, their son in the "demilitarized zone" (surely the cruelest misnomer in a cruel and corrupt war glossary), John, Jerry, and Carol and the children. And then I think of all our friends who are in prison, because of the same love which brings me here.

For them, love is a gravitational pull, the harsh routine of captive animals. And for me, it means a trajectory to the ends of the earth. *Benedictio Dei;* I declare a love which begins with my own family and which dares not end there. It ends where life ends, or nearly ends—in North Vietnam, the cheapest market of rags and bones in all the vast junk-yard of the absentee landlord.

We went together to the Chinese Embassy to begin conversations about an alternate route from Vientiane to Hanoi. Perhaps it was possible, as British airlines assured us, to travel through Peking? GRRR!—or whatever the dragon says through his teeth. Contempt, xenophobia. A small payment for the long compounded injury of maltreatment, "yellow peril," encirclement, overflights, exclusion from the world community, etc., etc.

We went also to the North Vietnamese Embassy. The men there could not have been more courteous. Their manner is hard and small and gentle. We came to ask permission to enter Hanoi during a week of humiliation of the Allies. Westmoreland had announced his usual body count. He has been perhaps the most persevering big- and small-game hunter of the century.

The little men sip hot tea with us, and, except for one brief flash of triumph, are too humane to rake over our losses. Time has gone over to their side, in the night. And with such an ally fled from us, what indeed is left to us? For you cannot import a guerrilla—you can only be born one.

On Friday, the Laotian Army dragged in the corpse of an antiquated bomber from the jungle. Evidently it was of Russian origin, and had been downed by the government forces. The wreckage resembled the opposite number of the yellow submarine. It was as though war, which is so seldom absurd, so often tragic, delighted for once to send us this unlikely heavenly visitant. The kids assembled in the park where it was displayed, like flies around a honeycomb. They climbed in and out of it as though it were some beneficent animal form. Meantime, nearby under a tent, the government was displaying the sorry remains of the sorry expedition: maps, the leather briefcase of the pilot, stained with oil and blood. As far as one could determine from the wreckage, the floor of the plane had been pierced with three or four tubes about four feet long. It was through these that the primitive rockets had been launched on the village.

Yesterday we had an interview with a Pathet Lao leader.

Two hours of rhetoric, grandiose accounts of the achievements of the guerrilla forces. This gentleman is left high and dry here with a small force of soldiers in the midst of the city; the phenomenon is a relic of an earlier agreement reached in Geneva in 1964. In virtue of this, a coalition government provided for four Pathet Lao memberships.

But after all the sound and fury, what comes through again and again from such a man is an unassailable conviction of the rightness of his cause in time and place. A readiness, as he declares, for every sacrifice, for a long war, for death and delayed outcome. This astonishing passion is almost totally lacking in the dead looks of the leaders who confront us at home, and the uncivil servants who greet us here. The Americans seem to gasp for air in the waters of a tank already infested with death—and with new life. A like danger.

At lunch on Friday we spoke at length to a Frenchman who had been a special policeman for the Emperor Bao Dai. He described how the North Vietnamese convoys escaped American bombers on the Ho Chi Minh Trail. (He had left Vietnam when Diem was rounding up enemies, and had escaped by jeep through the night with his family into Cambodia.)

He told how the seven-ton trucks traveled down the Ho Chi Minh Trail, one truck per mile. As a result of this tactic the bombers never got more than one or two or at most three trucks. The convoys traveled all night. But perhaps even more important than the motor vehicles were the thousands of bicycles; they seldom needed repair, and could easily be trundled off the main road into underbrush, needed no expensive replacement equipment, could be handled by one or at most two men with as much as 350 pounds of supplies aboard.

(It seemed to us indicative of the meaning of the bicycle that we found one of them apotheosized in the Museum of the Revolution in Hanoi.)

Our friend also described how floating bridges along the Trail were dismantled by day and swiftly assembled again at night. He declared with a certain Gallic relish how the Vietnamese even erect painted bridges, which our bombers would destroy with great fervor, while the pontoons of the real bridges had been dismantled and hidden in sections up and down the river.

At long last, after a week of despair and hope and the cancellation of two planes, we took off from Vientiane to Hanoi at 5:19 P.M. Our aircraft was described optimistically as a Boeing 707; we were told that it was about thirty years old. There survive only three of these marvels on our planet. A fourth crashed on the same run about one year before; no trace of it has ever been found. Our flight was half filled; the complement included both children and civilians, Poles, Indians, and ourselves.

Five minutes after takeoff. The Mekong is below; a vast sprawl of water whose sleepy gods are placated by messy little shrines like pigeon cages along the banks. Like the Mississippi, the Mekong is capable of blindly breaking out in floods. Now, where it crooks an elbow in mid-Vientiane, there lies a great golden bar of sand, like the aftermath of a gesture of creation.

Below, the rice fields, the primitive villages. A misty tranquil day, in a country whose changes in light and temperature are never severe or sudden.

We have been circling the city for ten minutes, gaining our altitude. It is forbidden to move gradually into the air corridor. We must gain altitude and then take off like an arrow.

At 10,000 feet we can still see the huts at the center of the fields; the dikes going outward like cracks in a green crystal. *O doux pays!*

Cumulus clouds, a lonely sunset. "Nature is the imposition of consciousness on fact." The fact for us, as we go to

34

Hanoi, is the maelstrom of violence and death that have stained the country, while we trudged our dusty vacuum and awaited the nod of the powers. But a like scene, viewed from an airliner above the United States or Europe, might induce a reaction of an entirely different order; the contentment of the gods, empery from sea to sea.

The stewardess has just shown us the "*casquettes.*" There is one for each passenger in the racks overhead. "*Ce n'est pas drôle—c'est serieux.* . . . Twice we have needed them."

The pilot came along the aisle to chat with us. He had flown the same planes, he said, back in '54. He had been back on this Saigon-Hanoi run for the past two months. He explained that they had radio contact with Hanoi; that we had three hours from Vientiane to make it. Thereafter, the U.S. Navy, with its bombers, and the U.S. Air Force were free to bring us down. There would be a one-hour stop in Hanoi. He recalled how narrow a squeak they had before the bombers came in last October 27; it was announced over the radio that the supersonics were twenty miles away from Hanoi. He landed quickly, just made it.

We asked him about the difficulty of taking off from Saigon with the city in siege since the Tet uprising. He said that ours was the only civilian aircraft to have left; there was still heavy fighting at the airstrip.

The mountains rise to about 9,000 feet; the plane is at about 11,000 feet. The crew wants DC's introduced; there is no pressurization in the cabins of these crates.

Every day, before the bombing sorties, the pilot said, the American flyers are shown the design of this plane and its markings. Yet, he reflected dispassionately, one of these planes was shot down and no remains ever found.

It is now 5:30 P.M. We have crossed the border and are in North Vietnam. Congratulations Zinn, Peacenik, Soul Brother!

There is great interest in us on the part of the French crewmen and stewardesses.

Not yet death. This is a wait longer than Godot, longer than Beckett.

Darkness. The lights are flashing from the ground outside. Howard (my cherished brother and friend, and Old Testament man of heart and guts) is deep in converse, in his delicious fractured French, with a passenger up ahead.

The old craft is shaking in every rivet, like a clay duck before the trapshooters, the war game experts.

How long have I wished to share the common life, to be compassionate with men, within the same fear, the same skin, the same trembling and fire and ice, to mourn with the men who die and do not wish to die; to weep for the children.

The first lights of Hanoi, 7:15 P.M., the runway. Easy down. The lights of the antiaircraft nest shine full upon us: "just checking, bud."

Night Flight to Hanoi

In a bar in Vientiane
they said to us
like Job's mockers;
thanks to your own ever loving bombers
you may never see
the northern lights, Hanoi.

Then, by bat radar
we crawled that corridor
blind as bats,
a wing and a prayer.

Came in!
the big glare of a klieg eye
held us, hooked, death's open season.
We held breath, fish
baited, not landed.

Ended; the pale faces of flowers
said suddenly, out of season
something than death other, unuttered.

Exiles we went in
safe kept, cherished by strangers.

How to convey the atmosphere, that long and dolorous entrance into the destroyed city; the endless pontoons of the bridges replacing the bombed span; the desolation and patience and cold; the convoys, the endless lines of military vehicles and cars.

As usual the loveliest fact of all was the most elusive and insignificant; we had been received with flowers.

We were ushered, at about 9:30 P.M., into the austere napoleonic deluxe of the "Hotel of Reunification." Supper. We are instructed, "Sleep well."

An air-raid alarm. We went to sleep like children and awakened like adults to the boom! boom!, the guns of an Indian summer, courtesy of our Air Force. Howard appeared at my door, disheveled and primary in the half light, like a runner awaiting the shot, without his socks forsooth. In a few moments we had crossed the garden and ducked into the shelter. Howard was decently covered by a German who placed his own rubber coat over those extensive and defenseless lower limbs.

Later that day, and throughout the week, I could hear the chambermaids in the corridor, singing; the plaintive atonal music with which the meek of heart console themselves for life in the cave of ravening lions.

Song

The maids sing at their scrubbing
the cooks at the stove—
shame women; such lightness of mind
ill becomes; think rather on
Death   Judgment   Heaven   Hell

the names of the bombers
that bear in their skull
your names, memorized in fire.

Life under Big Brother's shadow seems to awaken the submerged virtues—courtesy, compassion, cheerfulness of spirit. I think of the accounts of wartime London, and the instinctive sharing of food and space. When we climbed out of the garden tomb this morning, a boy had a pair of sandals waiting for each of us.

How is one to convey the atmosphere of a city rendered alien as another star by the mythology of our words, by distance, by bombs? It was like stepping out upon the threshold of a new planet, and then reporting back to those whose lives and history and future had wedded them to earth. The city was bitterly cold. And enormously silent. One could stand upon a corner and hear with closed eyes the vast whisper, as though of a great loom, the weaving of the wheels of hundreds upon hundreds of bicycles. Almost no motors in the whole city. A bicycle for every third person. It was as though in a cave of creation whose overarching sky was a protective darkness, a new creation was in its first stages. History being woven by a people who refused to die.

The city awakens as early as five A.M., to cold, to the privations of a people under the bombs. We noticed the thousands going off to work, pausing only to stop at one of the workers' restaurants for a bowl of rice and a cup of scalding tea. Indeed rice and tea are the blood of life itself. We learned later that the government had made its pledge of honor that every man receive his ration of rice. In accord with this pledge, there are no middle men between the farmers and the consumers. The rice is literally a line of life between the government and those whose perseverance and energy supply the stuff of war itself—and of survival.

We passed at least three bookstores, each of them open

and crowded. By seven o'clock young people were gathered in great numbers in front of a cinema; when the doors opened they pushed in as vigorously as though they stood in queue in Paris, or London, or New York. It was an early showing of a film, before work began.

In the street. The blank walls of second and third floors are covered with slogans and pictures, done in the crude realistic style of "Marxist modern"; heroes of the war shouting great slogans of victory and reconciliation and peace. In a street-corner showcase lay the attaché case of someone burned to death in a northern bombing raid.

We wanted badly to wander by ourselves, but the danger was explained to us: we knew nothing of the location of shelters, and in any case we could be picked up by the militia since we were without identification.

People look at us with a certain curiosity; but we have yet to see on a single face a mark of animosity.

The hotel is bloody cold and damp. (I slept in ski underwear and socks and was quite comfortable.) A good breakfast; café au lait, two eggs, good bread and butter and apricot jam.

Such a delight; everyone asked about Philip on our arrival, and was happy to know he was my brother.

The four guides who met with us this morning are undoubtedly the same who will be with us for the rest of the week. They seem businesslike and sophisticated; speak good English; they learned the language by themselves, they said. It was they who met Muste, Dellinger, Hayden, and in fact all Americans who have so far come here. The same group went recently to Haiphong to greet the *Phoenix*.

Most of them started their careers in adolescence, in resistance groups under the French. I judge they are not so much a "peace group" in the American sense as a liaison group between the government and foreign visitors. Their political savvy and their knowledge of our society lead me to believe that they are probably in training for future political leadership.

After breakfast we met with them for the first extended exchange. They were courteous and to the point. They wished to present a program for the week, and to hear our reactions.

We began with a question. Zinn or myself asked: What is the idea of the government of North Vietnam in releasing these three men? Can you give us some light, beyond the mere announcement of the fact and of their names, which we read about in *The New York Times*?

(I am reproducing here the sense rather than the exact wording of their response. Our language difficulties were rather great so we compromised with a kind of mishmash Vietnamese-French-English.)

They said: We are trying to educate the pilots so that when they return to the United States they will be good citizens, and give up "the dark thinking of their clichés." They are being released so that they will become good fathers and husbands. These pilots have, as a matter of fact, committed great crimes against Vietnam. The release is being initiated by the sovereign Vietnamese people; but it is not separate from the good relations and the task of building understanding with the people of the United States. Indeed, if we compare these men with those who have burned draft cards in the United States, there is an enormous difference in ideologies. It is not easy to convince these men of a new way; long and patient explanation is required. . . . Will your committee at home demand publicly that these men not return again to bomb North

Vietnam? Can you act upon them, and upon other soldiers, in somewhat the way you have been able to persuade large numbers of young Americans not to go to war? Because if they should return to our country and fight here, they would have to be punished again. Is it possible, even, that such prisoners should eventually do something for the antiwar movement in the United States?

Continued: But you understand that even if nothing should come of our hopes through these men, relations between you and us remain the same. But we do suggest that your committee in the United States should raise its voice, so that if these released men return to Vietnam to fight, against all our hopes and our sense of the rightness of things, no harm will be done to the mutual confidence existing between your movement and ours.

(As I transcribe the above, I am struck by the strange mixture of naïveté and human confidence. It is always difficult to convey the taste and atmosphere of these exchanges to our more sophisticated and war-weary American compatriots. But we were dealing with men who evidently had not lost all hope in the decency of the American public, a phenomenon which struck us as somewhat rarer at home than in North Vietnam.)

They asked us to express our preferences with regard to the use of our time in Hanoi during the following week. We spoke of our hopes of speaking with scholars and intellectuals and students, with people of villages, with city workers, and with representatives of the Catholic community. Zinn's wishes included government officials and political leaders.

(I am slowly getting a better sense of the identity of our hosts, the members of the peace commission. One is a graduate of a teacher's college, two are professors, and one a practicing musician.)

The streets of Hanoi, like a vast billboard; the banners that are shown in the photos and newsreels from China are evidently popular here also. We asked our hosts to translate the dominant ideas of the messages strung across city streets and emblazoned on the walls of buildings. It seemed to come to: "Congratulations to our brothers of the National Liberation Front for their brilliant victories of the past two weeks in South Vietnam."

A lovely lake marks the center of the city; at its heart is an island crowned with an ancient medieval pagoda. The farther end of the lake had been a target of bombing some months before and a number of children had been killed there. But the marks of the raid seemed pretty well erased; all kinds of trifles—pocket combs, mirrors, shoelaces, plastic utensils, caps and hats, socks and handkerchiefs—were on sale at a streetcar stop at the far end of the lake as we rounded it. And all along the banks, the potholes of individual shelters, each with its cover neatly laid half on and half off, like a teapot ready for the steeping. Then the communal bunkers, thrown up from soil and debris laid over concrete shells. I climbed into one of them and got the cavernous feel that I remembered as a child in the root cellar on the farm. A smell of damp, a sense of the absolute cold that lies at the heart of things.

The hotel atmosphere is something else again. Evidently the place was built toward the end of the last century or the beginning of this one, a kind of mausoleum of halcyon French hopes. Now it is filled with bustling, stern-faced, silent East Germans, Czechs, Hungarians, and Cubans. Amenities; a rather desolate-looking bar at one end of the lobby, knots of chairs and divans from the affluent era, several beautiful potted miniature trees, the garish fluorescent lighting overhead, an impression that somehow niceties are being kept up to the limit of resources.

All in all, the people are doing extraordinarily well. One has only to summon the atmosphere of feverish "normalcy" of a typical public day in New York City, the violence and pace, in order to ponder the meaning of human resources and the *esprit* of both cultures.

A visit to the Museum of the Revolution. A surprisingly clever and thoughtful visual assembly of photos, dioramas, and wall prints, some sense of the tortured history of North Vietnam since its pre-Christian days. A heavy atmosphere, the horrifying omnipresence of violence, invasion, death.

Item: A twelfth-century Vietnamese prince evolved a book of principles of warfare against the invading Mongolians. Three principles: (1) place human considerations above tactical; (2) place flexibility above strength; (3) prepare for a long struggle. I thought that such a book could have been an important source for Mao and Debray and Fanon. It would be interesting to pursue this.

In the city, as we returned from the museum to the hotel, a dreamlike trance seemed to lie gently upon people and trees and animals. Along the way, like pachyderms awaiting their cue before a procession, the great fleets of convoy trucks; on the move as soon as darkness fell.

After supper an invitation to view a film on the life of Uncle Ho. It came through quite well, the spirit of his life with the people, no very heavy hand. A life emerged, cut to the bone, the life of a peasant, a man with nothing to sell except his capacity for living for others. A little unsettling; such art is within the capabilities of this people at the midst of their struggle. Quite Gandhian in spirit.

Imagine the Pope or Johnson or Kennedy moving among

the poor in such a way, allowing spiritual forces to be liberated around one, allowing one's life to become an act of confidence in life itself.

(I catch myself wondering at times, What will be the music I march to on my return? One must be modest even in his expectation of defeat. Will the Church and the public, with their incurable middle-of-the-road stance and their American mythology of prisoners, accept the larger meaning of this trip? Will they tolerate my saying what I think must be said about this people? We shall see.)

This morning a big packet of books as a gift. Most of them seem, to a cursory look, beyond my capacity and sympathy. Jejune, touching in a people's conviction (which of course need not be very subtle or well articulated in order to be genuine). One book indeed moves me. It is the copy of Ho's *Poems in Prison*. (We saw the original of the book in the Museum of the Revolution today. It is bound by hand, and preserved under glass. The characters, as I noticed, were Chinese. Evidently Ho used the language of his captors in order to keep the manuscript from being confiscated.) It seems to me that only a true revolutionary would keep a diary in the form of poems. Probably the writing of this book in prison, and the experience of living in a cave on his return, were points of great change for Ho. "Lenin Mountain" and "Marx Stream"; so he named the places that corresponded to his change of soul. And I think of Jesus in the desert and of Loyola in Manresa Cave; of Matthew Goodman, his passion for ecological balance, and his death on the Vermont mountain. How else shall a man construct his soul, except he put on the universe for a body? Often it seems that exile and prison are the twin foci of inward renewal. The lake in the middle of Hanoi, flower gardens, the island floating like an open flower—all are parts of a great truth.

The only hateful or suspicious reaction we have met with has not come from the crowds in the streets. It was the face of a single foreigner of unknown vintage, which I remember with a kind of fear. He encountered us in front of the hotel and acted as though he could have struck us down with satisfaction.

We saw in the museum the darts and traps and home-made guns (one was a submachine gun made from railroad ties and modeled on the type Capone was making famous at the same time in Chi). I thought with absolute conviction that this was not for me, any more than the planes and missiles of the Americans. In both cases death, wounds, torture, poison. Though I must admit that the society here gives me more hope for the control and integration of violence than does our public experience at home. Is it possible that men may even violently defend an ideal, and in so doing come to moral superiority as human beings, despite the blood they have shed? Or is such an idea only the old lie in a new guise? Truly our present visit sharpens the debate on violence, instead of solving it.

Hatred of the French. Have we ever seen a more shocking and immediate evidence of colonial perfidy than that preserved in the photos of the "deals" made by the powers after Potsdam; by Japanese, English, French, and Americans? The museum in fact seems to me a kind of equivalent to the museum of atheism that we saw in Leningrad, a display of Orthodox and Roman Catholic sins. Nothing historical is gratuitous. If a whole people erects such a monument, it is because a historical sin cries out for vengeance.

In the museum, they have a diorama of the cave and

stream where Uncle Ho hid out and pondered his future on return from prison in China. Also a wicker handbag and two small pots, all his possessions. A camera shot of his house today, forty years later, showed not much more in the way of worldly belongings—two suits of clothing, two pairs of sandals, a small overnight case in a cupboard. Contrast this, say, with the white Mercedes Benz of the International Control Commission ginks in Laos. Ha! how to be (and not to be) historically at large! Vatican papers, please reprint.

The diorama of Ho's mountain retreat was, as I remember, the only three-dimensional exhibit in the museum. Behind glass it looked something like a Bavarian pastiche —hillsides, cement, paint, the skies and streams—for the birth of Christ. The merest alteration of figurines would have done it all. And the preserved diary somewhat like a fresh Dead Sea scroll. One is reminded of all sorts of relics and remains of saints in the churches and museums of Europe. What is a saint anyway, in a Marxist setting? And is Ho avuncular enough to laugh at his own apotheosis? They already have in public possession everything of his history—save his corpse. Only death remains to perfect it all; the tomb, the lineup of pilgrims, the admission charge, and, within, the gas-preserved corpse. How much more sensible and logical it would seem, in the light of revolutionary truth, to invoke the Gandhi "solution," the sprinkling of ashes on the Ganges.

A few simple truths carry a man through. All the rest is a lie. And the truth, even when a man dies, makes him in death all that his life refused him—a beacon for others.

(I am astonished to gaze in the mirror and find my bones suddenly transported from Cornell to Hanoi. Still I reflect; my surprise is that of a simpleton who has never troubled to prove anything, and yet who was proven not entirely wrong in the breach.)

Tonight they put an old electric heater in my room, somewhat like the one we used to "take the chill off" in the wintry rooms at home some thirty years ago. It chatters and sputters; the connection is faulty. One dares not get into bed and let the thing burn. Outside, flashes of noise like summer thunder, the sound of antiaircraft at some distance.

The French in Vietnam. They were able to raise perhaps the most formidable cultural epoch of modern times, here and in Asia and Africa. Something like Egypt and Greece in their own day. Yet I have never felt full in my face such a furnace blast of hatred against any nation as I have felt here against them. Was the Old Testament right? Are Babylon and Tyre raised inevitably on the mortise of a victim's bones?

(What Christians have to offer both to assailants and victims is a decision to go to the heart of the conflict, not as a solution of force, but as a solution of nonforce. If this is a Gandhian insight, so much the better.)

Instructions upon return. Develop for the students the meaning of Ho's "useless years." The necessity of escaping once and for all the slavery of "being useful." On the other hand; prison, contemplation, life in solitude. Do the things that even "movement people" tend to despise and misunderstand.

To be radical is *habitually* to do things which society at large despises.

The day was passed in the company of a certain Colonel Lao; spit and polish, genial, a little self-conscious in his spiffy uniform. He was Vietnamese representative on the war crimes tribunal, had worked for almost a year on the commission in Vietnam, and had attended the Stockholm tribunal. I was to see the colonel again; indeed Americans would have reason to remember him. *The New York Times* for May 7 carried his picture; on arrival in Paris he was to be second in command of the North Vietnamese delegation to the preliminary talks.

Our six-hour exchange. Perhaps one should not dignify it by a word that does not express what we endured. He began by expressing, with typical Asian tentativeness, his understanding that we were perhaps quite well acquainted with the history of his country leading up to the American invasion. Zinn was of course able to give an unqualified affirmative nod, I somewhat less surely. But no matter. The colonel proceeded with a three-hour monologue on the basics of Southeast Asian history, as these touched on the Vietnamese people since the first war of independence in 1945 and the strikes against the French in the major cities. Zinn was, as always, my Old Testament example for patience and long-suffering.

I stole glances out of the corner of my eyes at him to reinforce my own failing patience. And I would see him glancing with every indication of profound interest, nodding his head, as though the chichés and well-trodden facts he was hearing were indeed insights of the most profound character. It was only now and again, like land-

50

marks of hope on a painted ocean, that a bit of humanity would force its way through, and the officer would strip the epaulets from his mind. (Thus: the colonel is from Hue. His mother is still there, he has had no news from her in ten years. "*C'est la drame de notre pays.*")

In 1955 all exchange between North and South was cut off by the decision of the United States. An expediency of the Geneva Agreements was made into a political *fait accompli*. At this time even the postal exchange was cut off. All political and sentimental relations were ended. Two separate and tragic halves of one nation, wound meeting wound. Item: The postal exchange was at that time limited to five lines on a postcard. And even this pitiful concession was canceled in 1958.

I remember taking notes something like this, like the private graffiti of a court scribe on the edge of his official text. "God, how I wish he'd get on with something." Zinn's eyes and mine are slowly going backward into our heads. Two or more hours have gone by, I have downed two glasses of *eau de vie*. Even our hosts are nodding in their chairs, in the cold.

Precisely at two hours and twenty minutes by my frozen watch, Zinn was finally able to interpose a question, like a Dutch boy's finger in a cracking dike. Question: Is the "Front" to be the only governing body in a reunited Vietnam? The colonel: Let us say it is the only organization that can represent the aspirations of the South Vietnamese people.

He proceeded on his single track. Said: From 1965 to the present, the long-range plan of the American aggressors has not changed. But their form of aggression has extended further and further. Before 1961 one could speak of economic and social measures against our country. But from

1965 the word was war. Before '65 the method of conflict was one of sabotage; in fact the Americans sent a sabotage squad into North Vietnam and it was captured here. They flew in a C-47 from Saigon with troops and commandos. Their policy seemed to be, use the local people whenever possible. Also they waged a strong peace offensive at this time; an example was Johnson's Baltimore speech on April 7 of that year.

(Pinned over the window curtains are detailed maps of Saigon and Hue, with the plan of last week's attack outlined with arrows. Does this indicate the close collaboration between the North and the Front? Is it true that the whole campaign was planned here in Hanoi by Giap?)

The colonel: But the winter of '67–'68 has been marked by complete American passivity in the face of the Vietnamese forces. The dry season is now four months old but there has not been a single United States offensive worth speaking of. Yet a year ago at this time the aggressors launched "Junction City" operation on the sixth of February, with 45,000 troops. At present it is clear that they can no longer concentrate their forces, and are capable of defensive efforts alone.

(A long to-do followed, purporting to be analysis; but there was nothing new as far as I could judge. "Aggressive war," "imperialistic aggression," "heroic Vietnamese," "counter-aggression and brilliant victories," etc. etc. We become more and more restless, the smiles are more sternly fixed, even the peace people are tapping their watches and looking into the middle distance. This oral exchange reminds me of the Moscow harangues we endured, a peace group and the "cultural exchange" hacks, in the summer of '64.)

Colonel: The Americans lack the irrepressible strength

of the Vietnamese people, determined to fight until the end. Our great experience in the resistance against the French is standing us in insuperable stead. Even with a thousand times their present troops, the Americans and their southern mercenaries could not win; if they doubled or quadrupled their forces, it would come to nothing. And we make these claims as a small nation of 40,000,000 people.

Colonel, continued: Forty thousand were annihilated last week in the South and 100,000 were scattered and disintegrated as a fighting force. The Americans have tried to legalize the sending of their troops by saying that the Saigon government has requested their presence. But the very existence of the Saigon government is a violation of the Geneva Agreements. Because of course that southern regime should have endured only until 1956, when the country was to be reunited after general elections.

Said: If the war were fought along set lines, then the doubling of American troops might make a difference. But in such a war as this, the doubling of troops or their trebling or quadrupling, for that matter, makes no difference whatever. The enemy simply cannot hold "place." They must spread their troops so thin that their entire presence is dissipated. Moreover the terrain is entirely against them.

(The colonel is hottening up. This begins to become interesting.)

Said: In this war our people have no war theorists or "experts" at their disposal. But in the last couple of weeks, by the most simple of methods, they have been able to surround completely, with a guerrilla cordon, every place the Americans had claimed. The Americans have been harassed and entirely limited in their movements. And when the Americans dared to move against them, the guerrillas simply could not be found. They melted into the people. And of course the Americans had had no advance knowledge of the attacks, proving once more that the guerrillas are of the people. Only consider: twenty-seven cities and towns have been attacked in the course of twenty-four hours. The Americans could in fact be compared to a blinded and deaf giant. He sees and hears nothing.

Colonel: In a guerrilla war, the people are mobilized, the army in fact *is* the people. Every kind of weapon is used: cross bow, bamboo spikes, booby traps, and modern weapons also. The spirit of the people is the decisive factor.

Continued: In July of '66, Uncle Ho stressed once more to our people the theme of freedom and independence and the deep hatred which is aroused against the aggressor.

Said: You have been guilty of a grievous violation of the peasants' love of the land. The people have been uprooted from their countryside, and sent into concentration areas. You have heard of the one village, Ben-Suc; this is only one example among so many. With those great machines of destruction, the B-52's, operating on 10,000 sorties, with thirty tons of bombs per plane, one can quite simply alter the landscape to the degree that people who return after the bombings cannot recognize the place as their own.

Continued: One must speak of napalm, forbidden by the Geneva Convention of 1925. Yet this weapon was used this past week against southern cities, cities that only four days previously had been under the control of Americans.

Said: One must speak of the new gases, both those called D.M. and C.S.; 700,000 hectares in the one year of 1956 have been defoliated. It must be stressed also that this gas affects pregnant women, and leads to abortion and damage of eyesight. Gases such as these have been used frequently in so called mopping up operations. These gases can even kill people. Three American GI's brought evidence of the use of these gases to the Stockholm tribunal.

Said: The uprooting of peasants in the strategic hamlet program must also be called a war crime.

Said: And to speak of the North, all of our six cities have been bombed. Nam Dinh is almost 70 percent destroyed. Vinh is totally obliterated. Hanoi has been struck again and again. In our chief port, Haiphong, many areas lie devastated.

(He offered documentation of the War Crimes Commission at this point.)

Continued: We must speak also of the destruction of our hospitals. In thirty provincial towns, twenty-seven hospitals have been attacked; many have been completely destroyed. There have been thirty-nine separate air attacks against our largest leprosarium, a center for treatment against this disease and research. The hospital complex lay in a remote place; there was no conceivable military target around. Even after a warning and an appeal to your government, the attacks continued.

(And so on and so on. It amounted to a method of warfare by deliberate terrorism. The Germans have had very little advantage on us.)

(There followed a part of the interview which I shall try to summarize here.) This man truly brought the long day, toward evening, to new life. Evidence of genocidal intent and execution was beyond any reasonable doubt. The officer spoke of the killing of fisher folk who came to repair a dike that had been destroyed; another group of fishermen were attacked at evening as they beached their boats, and their wives and children came from the village to meet them. The aim is evidently the destruction of industrial, social, religious, and educational fabric of a society.

In the face of all this we thought of the prisoners, and could understand their release less and less.

(Two and one half hours this afternoon rubbing our noses in the fact and meaning of death. The colonel spoke of the deliberate experimentation policy, the new weapons used upon the Vietnamese people. Everything, in the course of three years of air warfare, had been improved— from airplanes to antipersonnel bombs.)

N.B.: Department of Folkloric Intelligence. Our meetings this afternoon are being held in a former home of Madame Nhu.

At one point of our interview we were interrupted by an air warning. We walked immediately to the shelter in the backyard; and I saw there, as I rounded a corner underground, three beautiful children, like a frieze against the wall in the half darkness, come to life, the children eating in supreme calm their dishes of rice, the oldest girl feeding the smallest child, her brother.

Children in the Shelter

Imagine; three of them.

As though survival
were a rat's word,
and a rat's end
waited there at the end

and I must have
in the century's boneyard
heft of flesh and bone in my arms

I picked up the littlest
a boy, his face
breaded with rice (his sister calmly feeding him
as we climbed down)

In my arms fathered
in a moment's grace, the messiah
of all my tears. I bore, reborn

a Hiroshima child from hell.

During the rest of the afternoon the colonel continued to
insist on one issue; one which was perhaps the strongest
legal point available. "The war at present is the only way
open to us, to implement the Geneva Agreements."

A tough, long day.

In the evening they showed us a beautiful movie. I think
they realized how bushed we were. The movie had to do
with folk customs of the mountain tribal people and their
dancing. Its change of rhythm made the horrendous psy-
chological battering of the day somewhat tolerable. And so
to bed.

The following morning took us to the former French St. Paul's Hospital, a large U-shaped building with a front garden, a wall, and a statue of the saint. We entered, to be greeted by Dr. Tiu, the vice-minister of the National Health Service, and Dr. Phan Van, the director of the Surgical Hospital. The latter proved to be an extraordinarily interesting man who had received his surgical training, as he told us later, in the jungles during the resistance against the French.

It was in the air. We were evidently going to get it again, chaps to navel. I shall do my best to underscore the high points of an extraordinarily difficult three-hour session. Indeed, what can it mean to ordinary men, endowed with ordinary resources of compassion, to view the overwhelming evidence of the death-dealing power and will of their own government? The question remains to haunt and appall us.

What followed that morning came in two parts. First, an hour-long report on the medical progress since the end of the French occupation. Under the French, 90 percent of the people, according to the director, lived in the countryside. There were no medical aid stations. It seemed natural to a colonial regime that there should be only one doctor for every 180,000 people. It seemed natural that there should have been forty-seven inadequate provincial hospitals for some twenty million people, and that in the ordinary villages there should have been no medical help whatsoever. However, in 1945, with the independence, the new government took up the enormous task of building adequate medical structures.

After the Geneva Agreements in 1954 the government issued certain directives to aid the growth of medical facilities. So today about 6,000 villages in the North and in the Delta have medical stations, and in the mountains 90 percent of the villages are now so equipped. The wide network of medical facilities was, according to law, to be extended to factories and schools and offices; the policy made clear the government's intention to serve the working people.

(According to their definition, a medical station exists in order to improve general health conditions, to give vaccinations, to examine people in dire need, to deliver children, to teach the villagers methods of controlling disease, to examine young children, and to encourage the growth of herbs and medicinal trees. Each center includes the services of three or four nurses and midwives.)

There was a heavy emphasis in the lecture and in the statistics on the well-being of the minority mountain tribes. Along with women and children, these people seem, in the official attitude, to be crucial to the future of the country.

Two practical examples of improvement of health conditions followed.

There was talk first of an improved privy, of which a model sat in solitary splendor on the table before us. The genius of the method, as anyone could realize who has visited or worked in developing countries, consisted in breaking the immemorial disease cycle between human elimination and the crops and fruit trees nourished by human faeces spread upon the fields. According to the new plan, after every use of the privy, ashes were sprinkled over the faeces and all dampness and germs removed. Eventually, when the manure was spread upon the fields, it was odorless and germless.

They presented the model privy to Zinn and myself.

The gift moved me, poetically speaking.

Progress in Rural Development: A Lecture on Privies, and a Gift to Our Countrymen

In the municipal hospital, in the bone-chilling cold
the dispassionate voices, Viet and English, unfolded
an invincible case for improvement of village privies.

Doubters, we sniffed with our senses the odorless faeces
achieved by new methods of drying. We stood.
The photographer readies. Passed to the doctor's hands

and to ours, and on through ten thousand miles
into marveling America (and carefully constructed
as a boat in a bottle, as a model of Model T)
              that gift, that two-seated wonder.

A new kind of village well had also been contrived; wells free of disease and diseased water were now in use in most villages; a well for every four or five families.

(There followed a series of movies in which a succession of horrors committed against medical facilities was repeated, one after another, with a kind of enervating sameness. The details are of no great moment, except as they would assure us that the attacks upon medical facilities lie beyond the scope of explanation based upon error and chance. Some 248 attacks have destroyed some 127 major medical installations. This includes 24 major hospitals, 39 district hospitals, and 54 other sanitary installations. Every attack seemed to have a single-minded plan. The planes always separate over an urban area; one group attacks the city itself, another concentrates upon a hospital area. The visiting team from the International Crimes Commission declared that they had never seen such destruction as has been wreaked upon the medical facilities of the North.)

I am quoting what follows from my notes, scrawled in the changing light of a film in progress, in a hand shaking with emotion and shame. As I wrote I felt like a Nazi watching films of Dachau. On and on, a record of perfidy and extermination. Leprosarium, TB hospitals, lying-in hospitals, general hospitals, medical stations. Destroyed, destroyed. A hospital in the vicinity of Hanoi destroyed by cluster bombs, some three hundred beds in complete ruins. Only five provincial hospitals remain untouched. It must be stressed that most of the hospitals are far from any other population centers. The only conceivable purpose of the attacks is to maim and kill the patients, and to induce terror in the medical workers, in order that the entire society might be intimidated.

The Childrens' Hospital on the outskirts of Hanoi is in ruins.

The attacks on the hospitals usually follow a general pattern. The first wave drops the larger explosives. A second wave sprays the survivors with fragmentation bombs. The purpose seems to be to ensure that North Vietnam will never again have sufficient medical facilities for a civilized future.

The first bombing of the largest leprosarium of the country was in December of 1965. The 2,600-bed hospital has now, after two years of repeated bombings, been destroyed and is in complete ruin.

The hospital destruction has included shelling by the Seventh Fleet, the use of explosives and CBU bombs, and phosphorus bombs; all have resulted in the wide-spread killing of patients and medical workers.

The air war has induced a profound change in the medical structure in the North. Now former hospitals are broken up into smaller medical units. Children are born, patients are operated upon, the victims of bombing are treated medically, all in smaller underground shelters.

There followed a heartbreaking summary of four "classical" cases of wounding of civilians by CBU bombs. The director of the surgical hospital conducted this surgical experiment, upon us. We were allowed to see in some detail, in the medical explanation, the X-rays of four victims of "antipersonnel warfare": a child of ten years, a young woman twenty-three years old (a teacher), a girl of twelve, and an older woman about fifty-five. It would be to no profit to give medical details here. These were exemplary cases of those who, in schools or streets or backyards or homes, had been wounded in the course of massive antipersonnel bombings. The teacher had some two hundred pellet wounds on her body. The boy had suffered the death of his younger brother and his father. The teacher and pupil had been wounded in the course of an ordinary day of school.

We can testify that these patients exist as described; we went from the X-ray lecture immediately to visit them, where they had been brought to one room in order to be viewed. We returned to the room for another cup of scalding tea; the hospital was murderous cold.

In the course of the following conversation it appeared that the following five rules have become generally acceptable as principles upon which medical reform and renewal are based.

1. All medical doctors must be skilled in first-aid methods.

2. All specialists must be in contact with other branches of medicine.

3. Medical workers must actually live among the people and share their lives.

4. Medical workers are obliged to turn difficulties into medical advantage and advance.

5. Medical workers must search out the simplest methods of dealing with the cases before them.

The above rules are hereby dedicated to the American Medical Association. We serve notice also upon those distinguished gentlemen that Zinn and I gave the North Vietnamese as accurate an account as we could of the appalling, overconcentrated, overdeveloped, overspecialized, morally inadequate, unimaginative medical establishment in force in the United States. We recommend to those Brahmins who are preventing adequate medical development in our country, and who internationally form a powerful cabal of money and property, inexorably opposed to medical reform, that they take notice of our report of them to the North Vietnamese people. We spoke of the hypocritical and miniscule "advances" represented by Medicare. We spoke in loveless detail of medical conditions in Harlem, in parts of which the death of children is as acceptable a fact of daily life as it is in the least developed country of Africa. We spoke of the inability of the poor to obtain medical care, when the circumstances of life itself produce disease and malnutrition—a systematic method of destruction of minority peoples in our ghettos. We said that, for all the rhetoric emanating from the White House and from the local units of medical monopoly, there has not been added a single medical school to the inadequate network of centers for preparation of medical doctors—many of whom are in any case hell bent on the corrupt benefits of overspecialization.

(The windows of the hospital, as the windows of every public building in the city, are covered with paper designs glued to the windows in order to prevent the fragmentation of glass in the bombings.)

The morning exposure to medical realities closed with the customary ceremonies, including, as usual, an emotional exchange and messages to the American people. To us these greetings often had the air of a Stalinist first-generation simplicism. But something came through beyond this, and met our hearts in mid-flight. Ceremony or no, truth or no, it was invigorating and even shocking to hear expressions of great love for national authorities expressed by their own people, as we did repeatedly that week. "Our leaders live the life of the people and do not work for their own interests." A working principle of great simplicity and of great value.

"Many of our visitors have agreed that we of Vietnam are fighting not only for ourselves but for the whole world." Again, a sentiment which we found to be both moving and accurate.

Again and again we heard distinctions made between the American people and the "imperialist war-making powers." The speaker often sends greetings to his opposite number. In one case, for instance, to medical workers and their families. And especially "to the families of those who burned themselves in protest against the war. Surely such a protest is unprecedented in the history of the world and evokes honest and most moving response on the part of the Vietnamese people." Amen. Amen.

We were invited to spend the evening at a center where all types of American weaponry and bombs were assembled in one large room. I had the impression that practically all the Americans who have visited Hanoi so far have been exposed to this gruesome show. I am going to concentrate only on certain highlights of that evening, trying not to repeat material that has been published elsewhere, either in photos or text. The weaponry was assembled, we were told, to facilitate the work of the War Crimes Commission in preparation for its Stockholm Assembly. Certainly we were struck by the international character of those who met us there: Cubans, Hungarians, and Frenchmen, among others.

No American can be unaware of the charge that a monstrous and intentionally genocidal air war is being waged by our country against the North Vietnamese. The fact is that, after the northern air war of the last three years, one can almost trace a kind of "genealogy" of certain bomb types. For instance, the pineapple bomb was formerly included in a launcher bomb, which contained 360 of these smaller explosive units. And at the beginning of the air war each bomber carried four of these enormous launchers. It was possible at that time to saturate a ground area of some 3,000 by 500 yards with a killing hailstorm of flying pellets. At present, in the so-called improved version, there are 550 to 650 small spherical bombs in a larger canister. (Photos of these have been published in *Ramparts* magazine and elsewhere.)

At this point my heart almost fails me. I remember that evening, the moment I tried with notebook and pen in hand to tarry at the rear of the group, pretending to examine the mechanical evidence of wicked intention, hoping to be excused from the group as the others went forward among the exhibits in the room. There were organs and parts of human bodies preserved in alcohol; they showed sections of brain and skull and heart and viscera, the path of the pellet bombs as they had killed civilians; the bodies had been dissected and brought here for this exhibit. I did not think I could bear with this. But at the moment when I had made my decision, another decision had been made up front. The young medical doctor who was undertaking this part of the demonstration paused in his opening remarks when he noticed that I was not in evidence. So I received a summons, polite but imperative: "Father Berrigan, come up here please!" And so I went forward, to have my face and my eyes rubbed in the fact and the smell of death, along with the others.

The medical doctor who spoke seemed to me the most emotionally affected of all those who had opened aspects of the war before us. It was clear that he had been unable to perform the operations that resulted in these exhibits without a traumatic interior impact. And his anger and anguish showed forth, even from the foreign tongue. But I continue with my notes.

They have preserved here even the skin of the dead, to show the effect upon tissue of this kind of weapon.

We saw also a section of skull perforated by pellets. The surface wound was very small, but within (as we also saw in a preserved section of brain) the wounds grew much larger as the pellets had ricocheted again and again off the interior of the skull until the whole brain was crossed with ribbons. On the surface of the skull, though the entrance wound was very small, cracks went out in all directions, like the shivering of a windowpane by a bullet. The skull was fractured from within again and again in all directions, from the single entrance of the pellet.

One of the most difficult medical problems posed by the pellets is the difficulty of discovering the location of the pellet as it weaves its incredible, rapid, and chancy way through an organism. For instance, we saw how pellets had entered through the back; it was found later that they had come out through the chest wall. A human heart was penetrated from side to side laid neatly into two parts. On first examination of another patient, the doctor thought that the victim had endured a fall from a high place. One could see hardly a single specific wound on the skin of the victim. And yet the course of a single pellet as it traveled through the body was a distance of some forty-five centimeters; it had penetrated and detroyed the kidneys and liver, and had finally gone to the right lung.

On the body of a child we saw evidence of a fractured femur; as the doctor declared, even hunting bullets cannot do such harm.

The horror pictures of death and damage by napalm are already familiar. There is a kind of family line of napalm bombs, constantly improved. We are far advanced from the days of merely preparing jellied gasoline. The combination of polysterin and other chemicals makes the napalm both much hotter and more adhesive. The phosphorus and magnesium weaponry was also displayed in their effects upon human flesh. We saw a picture of the pitiful, crisped remains of a woman, burned to a twisted black remnant in the midst of which there remained only a patch of flesh as evidence of her unborn child.

The exhibit of noxious chemicals was less familiar to me, as my ignorance of chemistry is very nearly total. But the whole question of defoliation was brought up at this point. I learned of the wide-spread death of animals that followed upon the contamination of forest areas and rice fields. We saw preserved in alcohol the evidence of rotten fruit and vegetables. Another point of which I had known nothing was the use of certain poisonous chemicals against the villagers. We saw also gas masks and sets of instructions in English, issued to the GI's so that they could save themselves in case the chemicals should touch them. There was medical evidence that these chemicals affect the meat of animals, and the organisms of those who eat such meats. They also cause noxious effects upon respiration, liver, and stomach. I asked a medical doctor, a Frenchman, at this point whether or not it had been shown that these chemicals had caused death. He declared that they had. He spoke also of the unknown area of genetic effects upon the cells and chromosomes of the unborn.

Some 700,000 hectares of rice had been destroyed; there had already been epidemics and wide-spread starvation in the South as a result of this chemical warfare.

(These cursory notes cannot pretend to be a complete account of war weaponry or method. They are one man's reaction to an exhibit that could leave no one unmoved. A much more complete documentation of these weapons has been offered and is on record, in Stockholm and in the recently issued "In the Name of America" documentation of the American Clergy Concerned Committee.)

Numbed and appalled as we were on leaving that room, I think we knew beyond any doubt that America would be accountable to history for a genocidal war, in violation of every international convention from The Hague in 1907 to

Geneva in 1929 and 1949, on to the hot pursuit of the Nazi "war criminals" in Nuremburg.

It was in the light of these bitter hours that we were also led to reflect upon ourselves, and our place in the American resistance movement. Time after time the North Vietnamese insisted that our place, as Americans, was not in North Vietnam. Our visit could be no more than a kind of keyhole view of the horrors of the room, well hidden from the gaze of most of our fellow Americans. The real question for us, as they saw it, was our return to our own country. There, a long patient work of revolution and renewal must continue. An adequate peace movement could not satisfy itself with assuaging the sufferings of the victims, by medical help at the point of impact. The radical work consisted rather in staying with conditions at home, trying as best we might to work changes upon a society in which military victims were the logical outcome of a ruinous, power-ridden national ethos in the world at large.

I thought also of an eminent American churchman who asserted in the last months that it is probably a better tactic for the peace movement to concentrate upon "broad areas of United States tactical and diplomatic and military mistakes, rather than upon individual instances of cruelty or civilian destruction." I only wish he could have been with us on this night. Perhaps he would have come to a realization that it is exactly here, in the flesh of the innocent, that the true measure of the war must be taken. But this awakening remains impossible as long as mere diplomacy is used as a measure of our damaging presence in the world. The real point I would think is that world indignation is centering upon the fact of the destruction of the innocent, already documented beyond reasonable doubt, a bad news which has already sounded around the world. It is by now clear that high levels of decision in our government and military have agreed upon a tactic of assault by terror. The simple intention of decisions reached months ago and now in process of execution is the obliteration of those structures by which a society survives and moves forward. Moreover, in Vietnam, the tactic is not aimed at a society that may easily replace structures already well developed and diffused. The fact is that here "the Stone Age" is a very recent experience. It has to do with centuries of retardation in structural and technological development, enforced by the iron hand of colonialism. So we are attacking a people for whom the replacement of structures once destroyed is a most serious and difficult task.

Such a tactic we actually viewed in action; it is even now being pieced together out of the destruction of North Vietnamese factories, schools, hospitals, and churches. It must proceed from a rather thorough understanding of the meaning of underdevelopment in modern society. It has even been suggested that such a study, deliberately applied to the Vietnamese scene, is now carefully aimed at the annihilation of a successful example of twentieth-century revolution. For it is perhaps well known by now that the nations of Latin America and Africa are looking to North Vietnam as the most brilliant example of a revolution already in full process. For this reason it is of supreme import to the American system now in operation that such a revolution *not* succeed. It stands out too starkly against the dismal millennial landscape of India, against the manifest failure of Western methods of organization in South Vietnam; it stands as well against the corruption and inanition of much of Southeast Asia. The North Vietnamese example offers, along with the example of Mainland China, a disturbing instance of the possibilities of thorough, ruthless land and community reform. But China is for the present inaccessible to civilian and military methods, and its internal difficulties render it a rather mixed specimen of revolutionary success in the world at large. But Vietnam is vulnerable to weapons already at hand, and to other weapons which the war itself reveals as needful.

I must add my own conclusion before finishing with this part of the diary. Evidence is at hand that the air war against civilian and social structures has become a tactic for subduing and crippling the North, and bringing it to a table of negotiation. If this society can be brought to its knees, it will approach us in the acceptable guise of the conquered. But to bring this about it is becoming clearer that the air war will not suffice; something more thorough than the wave of block busters followed by the waves of indiscriminate civilian death—something more than this will be required.

This added element of destruction in the face of evidence that North Vietnam is more vigorous than ever can only be expressed in nuclear terms. But more of this later, in the interview with the Premier of North Vietnam.

The failure of almost three years of air war, together with the shattering events of the Tet week in February, these are inducing tremors of extraordinary intensity in society at home. Some 250 years of national history, of domestic and international conflict, have not prepared us for the possibility of so unthinkable a thing as defeat. Defeat, moreover, at such hands! Hands which are neither large nor well fleshed out, nor white, nor skilled in the multiple uses and misuses of technological power. It is not to be wondered at that two forces of pride, one of dismay at the death of young Americans abroad, and the sense, cold as the hours before dawn, that we are about to lose a war for the first time in our history—that these two have induced an unparalled deepening of national consciousness. Americans perhaps for the first time in their history are about to have their measure taken by those whose stature, by every Western standard, is less than our own.

Is superman about to yield his inflated size, and the conviction of his insuperable strength, before the actual measure of human beings? It is a moment of the greatest peril, as well as of the greatest opportunity, for the world at large. For the Vietnam War, as the North Vietnamese seem to sense, marks a great moment for the world at large. National pride, inflated beyond the limits of sanity and mutual survival, is invited by an act of generosity and reconciliation to rejoin the community of men. This is the opportunity. It is the chance for Polyphemus to discover a crucial truth of existence. His eye has not granted him sufficient grounds for viewing reality, and his great size has inhibited his own survival.

Opportunity and danger! the twin poles of our national history, which the war itself, in a lurid and murderous light, has illumined for us. Will the one-eyed giant consent to live with the humiliation of his size and his semiblindness in the real world? Will he consent to see what he can see, and to confess what he cannot? And will he consent, in those areas where he cannot see, to listen to those who can?

In any case it seems to me part of an enormous historical irony that the encounter between technological overdevelopment and brilliant but modest revolutionary liberation has occurred in the course of a war which no one wanted and almost everyone is stuck with. Vietnam: a strange and unexpected geography for such momentous happenings. But perhaps, when we search for reasons for the dark days that have fallen upon us, one truth, not heretofore available to Americans, or indeed to the "developed" postcolonial West, would emerge. It goes counter to the falsehoods endemic to war, and epidemic to this war. Information and misinformation, infamy, lie above fact, the Napoleonic dreams of generals, body counts, whole families of weapons developed and perfected in the course of a single war, these and all other data, and technological advances, must now yield before the simple truth. It is a fact of history, a fact of the headlines of the Tet week of February 1968. A nation as simple of purpose and as candid in its determination to survive as were the first ragged refugees and refusers of the 1760's and '70's, such a nation has prevailed against the England of the century. Whether we choose to call that England new or old is of no import. What is of import, as it seems to me, is that a nation that once stood in opposition to established power is now itself the most cruelly established of all powers. It clashes arms against a shield, and announces terms of survival or extinction in the world of man. By way of counter-ideology to world revolution it claims to dictate the pace, speed, and form which human survival and community will take. And this, of course, given the beauty and truth of human variety, and the differing scale of human timepieces and cultures, is simply a monstrous, historically intolerable claim. And being such a claim, it simply will not prevail.

In a situation like ours, no day can be said to end in the way it began. We had been wondering and wondering about the prisoners; when our first meeting with them would occur, where they were, of what they were thinking.

The day dawned dreary and mordantly cold. It was a "good day" by Hanoi standards; when the clouds lowered, it was unlikely that the bombers would come out.

Our first meeting of the day was to be with Mr. Ky, the head of the union of journalists in Hanoi. His responsibilities also included lecturing to various groups in the city; as far as we could judge he was a kind of wandering scholar. He said simply that he went to lecture when and where he was asked; he liked best of all to give lectures to the workers. (He was a member of the Lao Dong Party; the party had a strength of about one half million in all.)

(I sometimes find it difficult to separate the course of an interview from the course of my own reflections upon it. This difficulty seems to increase in proportion as the speaker himself is seminal, and is able to scatter around us the seeds of some liberation, of some light.

In what follows I will try my best to distinguish and to assign authorship of statements; but I am not at all sure that I can cut the loaf that cleanly.)

He began: You are Americans, and you are here and that is a very great thing. And in your homeland, the fact that poets appear on stage, reading for peace, and the fact that Johnson cannot, in spite of many years of effort, subvert the intellectuals—all this points to an enormous achievement for your society. It also points to the pernicious attempts of a war-making machine, the blocking off into an enclave of war of the best powers of civilization.

He quoted: "To me a good friend from afar is like ten thousand books."

He said: Life in wartime has become normal life here. It is only by normalizing it that we make it bearable for so long a time.

(I think what follows is my own reflection.) They speak of the failures of experts to give the world back to the amateurs. And in this regard I think of A. J. Muste: "Our need is for a foreign policy for children."

He went on to speak of the uniqueness of the socialist character of things in Vietnam.

(I thought of the deepening of human evil, and of the possible purification of that nationalism to which we have become accustomed in our craven way in the West. I thought of Camus: "A man is responsible for his face.")

He said: If our sense of pride rests upon that which is truest to America, surely you and we can hope that the majority will not support the war.

(I thought the following was remarkable.) He said: We do not attempt to estimate our situation by the number of planes brought down over our countryside. The decisive factor for us is rather the firmness and constancy of our people. Life here continues, our production is good, the agricultural output is steadily advancing, no food need be imported, our national goal of five tons of rice per hectare has largely been reached; more than one half of the Delta is now producing this extraordinary amount. And yet, in 1963, before the bombings, none of this was so; one would have been thought a dreamer for proposing it.

Said: The rice production is our main lifeline. And the effort expended in order to produce enough for the needs of the people cannot be underestimated; consider the bombings night and day, the fields filled with craters and shrapnel, a constant threat to the lives of the peasants. For you understand that we cannot install sirens in the open fields, and that therefore a constant watch is required.

He said: Mr. Johnson must answer for this; a grain of rice kills no one. And yet to grow it the peasants' blood must be shed. And so the peasants say, the rice fields are our battlefields.

(He went on to speak of a kind of mystique of the factory—something deeply thoughtful and, as far as we could tell, true to the facts. I summarize.)

Said: when the French were here, they took care to destroy all factories before leaving; they even carried off the machinery. Since 1954 we have built some one thousand factories. Their capital is a special and precious thing to us. It represents the frugality of the people, not their exploitation by foreigners. And therefore it must be said that the destruction of the factories is a great cause of hatred, because the factories are linked to our blood and bones. We think of cigarette factories (we were smoking while he talked), of match factories, factories for electrical products and medicinal needs.

He said: The life of our people remains very simple. They do not need a great many things. He stressed rice, pigs, and poultry, cigarettes, tiles, bricks and cement, gas, vegetables, salt. (It seemed to me a list of those fundamentals in virtue of which a new people emerges from the caves and assumes a new consciousness and a new place in the world. I could understand that a Marxist would dwell on the destruction of a factory in somewhat the same way as a Christian or Buddhist would speak of the destruction of his place of worship.)

He invited us to trace with him the results of one single bomb falling upon a people. The resources which were dissipated, the deaths, the loss of whole families, of workers, of children. So with enormous reason it is said that one bombing brings hundreds of social problems in its descent. How then (he asked) could a pilot push a button, since with one death hundreds of problems were left with the living? One must also speak of the disturbance of the ecology of a land that would never be the same.

He said: Nevertheless, we turn our suffering into strength, we have our sorrows but we do not weep.

We questioned him on the so-called third force theory of the South Vietnamese Buddhist monk Nat Hahn.

(His answer seemed to me equivocal. It also seemed frightening, in the sense that Dostoevski's Inquisitor is always frightening. That is to say I am fearful when the suppositions of one's life are extended into universal values, and it is simply assumed with a kind of humorless irrefutable logic that the other will fall in line with one's own version of human life.)

I quote as well as I can.

"Political power reflects a social basis. In South Vietnam the main contradiction is between those who are the victims and those who are the aggressors. The latter will choose to withdraw or to remain. This question must be solved first. Life simply does not permit a third tendency, that they both withdraw and stay. Thus, those who fear the Front, and yet want the Americans out, are in a transitional state. That is to say, they do not yet understand the Front. But when the Front comes into their midst and explains the truth of things, they will join. And this will include all sectors of the people."

Zinn questioned: The NLF say that they will be very

tolerant after the cessation of hostilities. But we recall that after 1954 many in the South had collaborated with the French. What happened to them?

He answered: May I answer with a parallel example drawn from the North? After 1954 it was clear that over one half million of our people, from villages to capital, had worked with the puppets. We came in from the jungle very impoverished. There was nothing in the banks or the treasury, and the lands which had belonged to the French were almost totally uncultivated. The average salary was about six dollars a month. Meantime, just before their withdrawal, the French had trebled the salaries of all those who worked for them. And we allowed those collaborators to stay on, and decided that their salaries should remain the same as before.

Yet those who worked for the new government earned on the average of six dollars a month. At the same time, for example, a porter whose salary had been set by the French would continue to receive about thirty dollars a month. And this continued for as long as four or five years after our revolution. Finally, those who had collaborated gathered together and petitioned the government; do not continue such discrimination as this—it is a shame!

It was the attitude of society itself that had helped them to change. For instance, Mr. Ky, our interlocutor, worked about sixteen hours a day, while most of the former collaborators worked about eight. But even then he wished to insist upon the fact that a solution came about by personal choice; those who chose could continue with their former inflated salaries; the question of money was not the first question at all. The important thing was that such men, along with others, could work and serve the people.

There was another question here, we believed, than the

question of literal truth. It seems verifiable that at least some of the collaborators were not treated in so benign a way. But in a sense the very fact that reconciliation to the new society would be seen as possible through a process of inward change seemed to us remarkable. It remains remarkable even though it remains an ideal. And it has, one would think, the widest possible implications in prison and parole work, not to speak of questions of public honesty.

(I am including these little Marxist homilies such as the one that follows because they reveal the kind of naïve faith in human goodness that is so powerfully operative in North Vietnamese society. Even apart from performance, I think they raise questions about one's belief in the capacity of men to undergo change.)

Continued: As Marxists-Leninists, we believe that you cannot confiscate a man's conscience. He must change gradually. So we have often left intact the material conditions of former collaborators, even for a period of ten or twenty years. In the same way we are not in a hurry in our opposition to the Americans; the war may continue for ten or twenty years. But what is that in comparison with the centuries of foreign aggression we have endured? Indeed we have a saying: To one who has traveled four thousand miles, ten miles more are nothing. Moreover, such puppet functionaries as we are discussing have been in their state of mind and their social condition since their birth. It would seem to follow that they cannot be changed in two or three months; so we let life itself, step by step, solve this question.

(We inquired as to the meaning that the word "democracy" holds in the Democratic People's Republic. I summarize the little discourse that followed.)

Continued: For us, the people are the masters and the

administrators must in fact serve them. For us, problems of law and the constitution are not primary; the real question is that of the dominance of the people in all fields— economic, cultural, and political. So, for example, in production the peasants make the decisions on planning and techniques. So also with the workers; they are masters from production to distribution of the goods. Let me speak of another example of what I mean. A child has the right to ten kilos of rice per month, a miner twenty-four kilos. This is plenty for the needs of each. But if for example I work better than another man, I receive more in salary, and may use my salary as I wish. But the least the regime can do for me is to supply my basic needs—which in fact amounts to the need of rice.

We questioned him with regard to standard of living and comparative expenditures. He answered in summary: the minimum wage is about forty dong (about six dollars) per month. Of this amount about $3.50 goes for food. About 1 percent of one's salary is spent on rent, water, and electricity. A minister of government or the editor of an important paper would receive about six times the minimum wage. Our President Ho Chi Minh receives about seven times the minimum wage.

In this regard they told us a humorous story: Our President once talked to a foreign journalist and the question was raised, Has your life changed very much since its early years? He answered, Yes and no. Forty years ago I was a dock worker in the United States and made about fifty dollars a month. Now I am President of North Vietnam and I earn about forty-five dollars a month.

(We noticed even in the short time we were in the North that there is a truly impressive liberation of women into areas of public responsibility. We asked about this.)

He said: In accord with the new constitution our women have gained their emancipation. For example, any enterprise whose constituency is more than 50 percent female must be directed by a woman. If this percentage is verified in a farming cooperative, the chairman of the whole enterprise must be a woman. In the average village council over one third of the ruling body must be made up of women.

(We asked about the meaning of democracy as it would apply to local participation and initiative.)

Responded: The principle is that there must always be exhaustive discussions before decisions are reached. For example, before the resolution on women became law (the law of which I have spoken above), three months of discussion took place. All the methods of war resistance, what to do in face of the expanded air war, methods of production, even tactics at the front, all these were roundly discussed in local councils. When finally a vote is taken, if many are still divided on two sides of the question, another discussion follows until unanimity is reached.

Continued: Thus also the National Assembly does not discuss all problems, but only the most important ones. But for these important questions the members meet in small groups and talk things over many times. As far as local discussions are concerned, they are based on neighborhood and on work teams. There is no age limit for voting on a resolution; in the farm cooperatives the children both criticize and speak openly on prevailing conditions.

Continued: The last election for the National Assembly was held in '64. A new election will fall due in '69. Our President is, of course, a member of the Assembly; out of the whole assembly comes his appointment as President of the country.

Question: Does capital punishment exist here?

Answer: Capital punishment exists in law but there has been no execution of a prisoner since 1954. During the war with the French there were executions based upon treason cases, but no execution of former collaborators. But those who were caught in overt acts of murder were put to death.

(Even though we had hopes of meeting with the members of the Catholic community, we wished to open the religious question with a Marxist. And so we asked Mr. Ky to comment briefly on religious conditions in the North.)

He made three points. I summarize:

1. Religion is a question of conscience and is never to be solved or resolved by means of violence.

2. We regard religious people with a "social eye." That is to say, they are workers, peasants, or intellectuals and from a social point of view they may or may not be our friends.

3. The religious question is an inevitable one in the course of history. One simply cannot suppress what is fundamental to man. At the same time, however, we insist that man should be marked by a patriotic conviction; one must participate in the work of building society. Some may disagree with communism in principle; we ask them only to join us in building the country. But no administrative measures can be useful in solving what is essentially a question of conscience. So we respect all beliefs.

Continued: Churches are bombed (by the "religious" Americans) and the government gave aid to reconstruct these buildings. In Hanoi we join the Catholics in their celebration of Christmas. I myself go to the cathedral at Christmas to share in their joy. And at the time of Mr. Salisbury's visit to us at Christmastime, I invited him to my home to share in our Christmas banquet.

Continued: Indeed a bomb does not distinguish a Communist from a Catholic. And many believers have joined in our revolution from the beginning. The Buddhist monks also helped; they hid many revolutionaries during our struggle with the French. And so, after the war, we never once entered their pagodas with army units.

(Somehow or other, in a way which is inexplicable to me now, the following delicious paragraph got included toward the end of Mr. Ky's discourse to us. I find its note of confidentiality and off-the-cuff bonhomie both engaging and terrifying. It was almost as though someone's uncle were confiding that there was a corpse in the potting shed; but that of course was all right, since superior powers were in charge, whose goodness could not rationally be placed in question.)

It went somewhat like this:

Confidentially, I will say to you that Johnson's aggression is being defeated. His military skill is really very backward. He cannot understand the meaning and force of the Peoples' Army. The Americans admit to a great surprise in the last weeks. We are in no sense surprised; but they are incapable of understanding us, so our natural mode of operating is a great shock to them. Imagine! over thirty cities attacked simultaneously, thousands of people involved; and where during all this preparation was the CIA? And I must add, there are many unexpected things in preparation for Mr. Johnson. So an early withdrawal would be a very fortunate thing for the American youth.

Continued: I have met your young people many times; and I must say that I love them very much. We fight them only because we are forced to do so. In the near future we must win our final victory; therefore there will be many more casualties. But how can we in all conscience avoid this? We have already undergone many years of suffering. And we cannot lengthen our suffering beyond limit for the sake of your youth. In spite of the love we bear for them, we cannot tolerate their aggression. So the real question is how to bring the administration to an understanding of this. How can we bring them to understand the facts of the war in a way which will benefit their own youth? How can we ensure that the resources of the United States are not squandered uselessly in this war? And how also solve the terrible burden placed upon our conscience by the temptation to excessive killing?

(I must say in all honesty that I find the preceding, as I read it over again in the rather less heated atmosphere of my university, a balanced examination of conscience. If such statements are to be smeared with the brush of "propaganda," then one must admit that this is a new form of propaganda, based upon an understanding of the horrendous waste of lives on both sides of the firing line.)

(I am setting down these notes toward midnight at the end of a bitterly cold day. We are to arise at five o'clock and proceed about forty kilometers to an agricultural cooperative. But I must set down a record of the extraordinary evening we have just finished with. It must be recorded, if only because it is the first evening of its kind to have taken place since the war began.) Tonight we had our first meeting with Methany, Black, and Overly. I write these notes less than an hour after the events recorded had occurred.

About six o'clock in the evening we were told that we could see the prisoners at about 7:30. We would meet first with representatives of the North Vietnamese military, to be briefed on the names and status of the men. So we proceeded toward midtown, to a kind of town house set in a walled compound. It was not apparent to us whether this was actually the prison, or whether the prisoners had been transported to meet us in this place. In any case, we drove through a pair of French-style gates, promptly on the half hour. We met first with the officer, his secretary, and his translator in a kind of anteroom. The meeting was, predictably, quite stern to begin with; but the courtesies slowly prevailed. The officer read off a series of facts: name, age, marital status and family, military unit, the usual information recorded on military identification tags. He then spoke of the meaning of the gesture of release in rather formal terms, as understood by the North Vietnamese Armed Forces. We had heard the same theme repeated often before in other sectors of the society. The release of the prisoners was, he declared, a gesture of peace.

We were then invited into the next room, where the prisoners would be brought in.

The seating arrangement went something like this, as I recall. We were all at three tables in a rough U shape. At the right, the army officer and his secretary and translator. In the middle, Zinn and myself and two members of our Peace Committee. And on the right the three prisoners. The tables were covered with cloths, and in accord with Vietnamese courtesy there were plates of cookies, tea cups, and cigarettes. First, at the curtained door immediately to our left, appeared a Vietnamese private; he saluted vigorously and disappeared. The prisoners entered immediately, the shock of the evening, the shock of the week; indeed, one of the great earth tremors of the war so far recorded on the sentimental seismographs of the West. These were the faces that had launched a thousand newsmen—from Tokyo, from Korea, from Bangkok. The airmen entered in single file, dressed in black pajamas, two-piece outfits, no socks, sandals. They marched in, stood in a row before their table, and bowed to the waist in the direction of their military captors. I was struck by the thought, How well they look, how ruddy, how clean cut, how unkillably American. They looked better than their pictures, better than us, better than the hundreds of thousands of people we have seen laboring and cycling through the streets. They look like Americans. They are identifiable and tall and broad of shoulder and narrow of hip; they look like the movie marquee figures in Vientiane, in Paris, in Johannesburg.

Zinn and I went forward and toward them, around the table, and shook hands, somewhat against their expectation; somewhat, if the truth were told, against our own.

We had been instructed beforehand to limit our talk to, first, greetings and, second, news from the states. No news of their families was to be given, and no details of our return trip to the States.

(Actually the instructions were not severe ones, since we had no news of their families, and since the manner of return was still under discussion.)

We all sat. The officer stood and came to the middle of the floor. He invited conversation between us and the prisoners; the exchange would last for about one hour. And so the prisoners began. They seemed eager and nervy and somewhat overanxious to please. They declared without prompting that they were well fed and cared for and grateful to the North Vietnamese military for the kindness with which they had been treated. (And here I am summarizing rather than reporting verbatim.) They said they had been given news of the war regularly, that they had visited Hanoi during Christmastime, that they had had a Christmas celebration "with a tree over in that corner there," that their Christmas dinner had consisted of turkey and rice, that they had even received a kind of gift package at that time. On Christmas, too, a Mass had been held for the Catholics and a Protestant service for others.

The major said something like this at one point: "I have had time to think and to come to new views. I would from now on take no day for granted." There was also a remark to the effect that the days had gone very slowly.

(What these "new views" of the major's were never became clear. What did become clear was that no real change of heart with regard to the moral questions of the air war in North Vietnam had occurred on the part of this senior officer. In fact his story, with its climax, the encounter with the American ambassador in Vientiane, forms a remarkable case history in the instance of seizure of the intellect.

(I have succeeded in enraging many Americans since my return by conceding that these men were brainwashed, and most especially this senior officer; they had been brainwashed by the American military. But more of this later.)

At one point our interview broke off as an air alert sounded. But it was the North Vietnamese military who dropped the bomb this time. The major arose, stopped our chit-chat with a gesture, and announced that the bombers were once more sixty kilometers from Hanoi. And that this outrage was "occurring while we sit here talking about peace and brotherhood." Then: "If the bombers actually loose their fire over Hanoi in the next few days, of course the release orders of the prisoners would be canceled immediately."

Given the long cold night sweat of the past weeks, given the long loneliness of the prisoners, awaiting us dur-

ing the days we were grounded in Laos, given the ambiguous meaning of their release and the continued imprison-
ment of their fellows, the announcement was indeed a
cruel one. That it was a just one also needs to be taken into
account. I told Zinn later how fervently I agreed with the
view of things announced in icy tones by the officer, as
death bore down upon the city once more, yet once more.
For as I saw it, the absolute issue of the trip was not our
returning with the prisoners, it was our having some effect
on the conclusion of a monstrous war. And my reasoning
(and my anger) continued in somewhat this vein; our
State Department knows that we are here in Hanoi. It
knows why we are here. It is possible that nothing more
exacting than a phone call to the American Air Force
would be required to urge reasons for going easy on the
bombing, at least for a few days. But if they wish to continue the air attacks while we are here, then by all means
and with all our hearts let us go home empty-handed—and
let us say why.

(It is, I hope, apparent that I am concentrating on only
one issue. For the truth of the matter is not solely that the
fate of three captured men hung in the balance. The larger
meaning of Hanoi under attack was the question. Three
lives, in the midst of a monstrous threat to life itself. They
were one instance, and perhaps the ambiguous instance, of
the savagery of air bombardments against a nearly defenseless people. But it seemed to me that our task was to
try, as best we might, to lead our fellow Americans from
their obsessive pinpoint concentration, sentimental and
even corrupt, on the fate of "our boys," into a consideration
of the meaning of the war itself, of which these men were
the triggers, and finally, to a degree, the victims.)

Our conversation went on for fifteen or twenty minutes

longer. After the sirens subsided, we walked on thinner ice, and with a weather eye open, uncertain of what unknown forms lurked below and above us. But the men seemed to warm toward us and to relax visibly. Black, for instance, made a big and almost immediate issue of wanting to convert to the Catholic Church. (This for my benefit?) His wife, he said, was a Catholic and he a Baptist. He had questioned me rather closely about whether I was a priest or a Jesuit and what difference there was between the two. All three men concurred in granting some rightness to the North Vietnamese in the war. It came down to this: "They were defending their country."

(The concessions would vanish rather quickly when the chips were down, as we were to find.) It is of course one of the most vexed tasks of the century to try to assign responsibility for actions during wartime. Since the '30's, the shadow of Eichmann, of Pope Pius XII, of Bonhoeffer, Delp and Jagerstatter have lain heavily upon our lives. Never again will it be easy to choose virtue or wickedness.

Would it for instance have made any difference in the lives of these three if, at some point of their experience in the air war, they had been led through villages, and had seen, as we saw, the effects of their weapons upon the bodies of children and women? Indeed we know that in many ways they had received the harsh and immediate treatment meted out to the vanquished victors of the sky. Two of them had been exhibited in villages and beaten by the peasants. The life of one of them had been saved three times from literal mob fury by the courage of his guards.

The three men are thus not to be thought of as descending painlessly from their murderous heights into a more or less protective custody. No, they struck the earth with all their bones; two of them had been severely wounded by the impact. Moreover, the major had spent some sixty days on the road, with stops for medical aid between the place where he was shot down and the city of Hanoi. The deep circles under his eyes and the lines of age and suffering about his mouth testified that his interior life had indeed undergone a tumultuous change; he was not a tourist to his own deeds. He had made his bed and been thrown upon it, and the bed was Procrustean indeed.

Yet I reflect, with a certain anguish and heaviness of heart, that nothing in the youthful training of this man had been seriously thrown off balance by these long and hellish months. When crisis came he walked out of the rags and sewers of his experience like a kind of secular Lazarus. He was restored in every limb, in every muscle and reaction, to his pristine literal vigor, the strength of the war-maker. I know no way to account for such a fact, except to appeal in a general way to the enormous deformative power of militarism and nationalism, when these enter the heart of a young person, purporting to reflect the truth of human existence and to evoke a response worthy of an adult conscience. The major responded at Vientiane, on Friday night, as a spotless knight—one of whom his country and his mother and family and very probably his church, and in the next ten or twenty years his children and their children—all would take pride in him. Pride meeting pride; unless by chance some genetic disturbance, in nature or biology, should occur. And that of course was not to be expected or counted upon.

The major's total integration into the modern state, the modern church, the modern family, as a thoughtful and respectable and honorable killer—that was the rub. It was the rub which would rub men out. It was the murderous normalcy of war, reduced to one man's life, and reflected in those dark eyes and their suffering, and their secret, and their silence, their waiting for the moment of "debriefing," the moment when the sacred confession could be launched in the consecrated ear of higher superiors—all this was the burden of our winter's tale.

My final poem of the week, written on the Air France flight from Paris to New York on Sunday morning, went in part like this.

The Pilots Released

1.
The trouble with innocence
is itself, itself in the world.

The GI who had a wife
but never imagined one
had children true to form,
whose lives described
like dance or geometry
the outer edge, drawn there
in the diametric blood;
thus far love, and no further.

I must set down a few words also, at least in passing, on the ensign, Methany. His was by far the most attractive personality of the three. He could perhaps be thought of as the classical son of that perennial mother named Whistler, if she were younger, somewhat less dark and gloomy of visage, and yet retained her ikonic quality in the hearts and lives of her countrymen. The classic son of a classic mother! And if there be any trace of cynicism in these reflections, surely they would be erased by one glance of that candid and anguished youth, only twenty-three years of age, who had undergone so much, and learned so much, in so short a time.

Was the trouble with him, the trouble which made him so much more perplexed and inward and unsure than the others, was this trouble merely his youth? He had been in the Air Force for only three years. A layman can only hope to imagine the quick reflex and intelligence required to ride those human bullets of which he was one of the skilled pilots. He was quick also in other ways, as he declared in the tones of his monologue during the plane flight out of North Vietnam. We were riding a slow, laborious aerial elephant, in some contrast to the manned missile of which he had been in such proud command some months before. And he could joke, like a railroad engineer trapped in a boxcar, about the old scow we were wallowing in.

He spoke of episodes in the camp, but only in an indirect way; he had reacted savagely to certain events of which he would not speak in detail. But it was clear that he had been punished; corporally, and in a far more terrifying way—by solitary confinement.

I conjured up this young life, confined to a single room except for meals and a weekly wash, confined to a single room for 104 days. The reality is indeed a terrible one. The more so because he was evidently gregarious and talkative; a man for whom the ear of friends was a necessity. His captors brought him out for frequent interrogations; he was given books to read and made to report on them either orally or in written assignments. But he confessed, with his indomitable candor, that he had found the books of great interest; they had opened a side of the war of which he had been ignorant. The books seemed to consist mainly of analytic studies of the war from a point of view of the American resistance. As I recall (and my memory of course may be faulty because the following is not in my notes), he seemed at one point to lean forward and gesture across the aisle to where Zinn was in conversation with the other two pilots: "And one of the books was his!"

But this youth of twenty-three years! There had been placed in his nervous capable hands, hands which seemed in their perfection the outward instruments of his mind, a terrifying power, a power over the life and death of others. And yet, limiting those hands, and the brain of which they were the instrument, was also a radical imposed powerlessness. For Methany, when all reservations were disposed of, and his perplexities vigorously swept aside by the imperative of other wills, Methany also was an obedient man. And that is nearly everything there remains to be said about him. It is his obituary.

But to speak of him in such terms is not in any sense to dispose of him. It may be, and one can so hope, that according to the repeated wishes of the North Vietnamese, Methany and the others will not return to North Vietnam as bombers.

And yet, and yet. It remains that there are thousands of Methanys; they crowd the womb of the Air Academy, clamoring for birth, clamoring for wings. They are, according to mien and intelligence and perception, the genetic triumph of our long biological experimentation. They have grown the new organs which allow us to control the skies of the globe. And being quite literally airmen, their organisms make whatever further adjustments are required in order to turn men into instruments of the upper air; speed and more speed; death is our product.

(As an airman remarked jocularly to us in Bangkok on our return, the airport buzzing like a hive of wasps with jets outside and airmen within, he was off to some base or another to pick up an "improved job." It was explained to me later that the "improved job" was a new type of bomber that would fly some 1,600 miles an hour. Up to then there were only a few experimental models at work on North Vietnam, but the number would be increased; their performance was satisfactory.)

What sort of proximity to actual war is required, if men are to become thoughtful and critical about their actions? We have had years of this war, clogging our television tubes and our heads with horror. In a true sense we are closer to the war than the airmen who are pursuing it with such savage vigor at the scene of conflict itself. And yet one could hardly claim that the eyes of men have wept for the victims because of what those eyes have seen. Indeed an opposite claim might be made; that one televised war has prepared our souls for all kinds of future horrors. I do not know which effect is closer to the truth, with respect either to ourselves or the freed airmen. I listened with a kind of ignorant amazement to their bantering, the kind of talk that goes on when men meet over athletic conflicts to celebrate their gamesmanship. The joking, as I recall it, had to do with the contest, like that of two ball teams, between the airmen of the fleet and airmen of the Air Force. Did it not say everything for the superior skill of the pilots of the fleet, insisted Methany with mock vigor, that they could take off and land upon the turbulent postage stamp of a carrier deck? The war game, literally. It was for

all the world like the humor attendant on a Sunday afternoon ball game in a small town. Did it arise by way of
relief—a saving relief from the killing war, the obedience,
the discipline, the chill omnipresence of death? Or was it
rather a form of ignorance, a way of saying that one did
not know anything of what one was doing, that one was
leading his life on a kind of green and lovely field, on
which the highest stakes were nothing more significant
than the playoffs, the final honor or dishonor, first or last
place—or something in between?

Methany spoke with deep affection of his father; a man
still in his early forties—something still of a brother and
pal. They went to ball games together. There was a deep
bond between them, which the months of separation had
only served, from the son's point of view, to strengthen.

The fliers were evidently the young Krishnas in our war
pantheon. The last frontiersmen of a war technology which
perhaps in ten or fifteen years will be able to dispense even
with them, as weapons' systems take control, and even the
most highly trained and motivated human beings become
unnecessary to an air war. But in the meantime their total
training is a witness to the fact that man has met the machine, and is still in control of it, at least for now. But what
man and machine are doing, what convulsing and over-
throw of the ecology and culture of a small, proud, and
ancient people—this is another question. It is a question
which the minds of these airmen, as far as we could learn,
were not so much as groping toward.

But to our Tuesday meeting. Were the three airmen
playing to the gallery, with their reference to Catholicism
and conversion, to good treatment, to gratitude, to bows in
the direction of their jailers? Indeed we made an enticing
audience, the priest and professor, the army man scrib-

bling away at his notes; so much in the balance, men in less jeopardy than these have been known to put their shiniest shoe forward. We will have to see.

Of very first import, as our hosts make clear in many indirect ways, is that we finish our mission by returning with the prisoners, all the way to New York itself. It goes without saying that Zinn and I are resolved that we will never take an army or state plane of any vintage or any degree of anonymity, no matter what the fliers decide. As we understand, it is of extreme importance to the North Vietnamese to be able to show that this operation was carried through by peace groups on both sides. Moreover, that the operation was effected despite the military powers of the United States. And with all of this I heartily concur. Moreover, it was the basis of our agreement with Dellinger and Hayden in New York. And finally, it should be stated for the record that both state and military had assured us in New York that our wishes, and the wishes of the airmen, would be respected.

For days we have been discussing alternate routes home, in case the Control plane is unable to get through on Friday. Neither Zinn nor myself are enthused about the Peking-Moscow-Paris route. But at least it has this to commend it: it would place us beautifully outside the United States' power, and make it impossible for the military to interfere with the pilots, even as far west as Paris.

But the answer to our real question is still unknown at this point (Tuesday evening): What will the three airmen want to do?

We have seen not even an hour of clear sky since our arrival. From the point of view of the Hanoi people this is a great benefit. No bombings. Dreary rain again all day.

A visit to the farm cooperative of Dan Phuong
(the village of the Red Phoenix)

We left the hotel through the cold morning for a trip of about forty or fifty kilometers into the farm commune. We had been promised a rather thorough treatment and hospitality. And by the end of the wearying and exhilarating day, Zinn and I felt that our hopes had not been defeated.

Through the bone-chilling air, we made our way gradually out of congestion and early morning energetic foot and bicycle traffic into the open countryside. Past the evacuated Schools of Drama and Dance and Ballet; all of them points of pride of development, all empty and dispersed in the course of the last year. They were the only really prestigious things on the landscape. For the rest, it was a matter of miles of shacks set up along the roadway, some of them shelters for workers engaged in government projects, some of them living quarters for peasants working in nearby rice fields. A sense of what might be called the intense, populated desolation of a war landscape. Multitudes of people passed us on bicycles and on foot, many of them heavily burdened; it was a scene at once of energy and of sorrow. And as always in a society that has made such enormous strides, a sense of the retardation and enormous damages induced by war.

We arrived, like explorers, into a landscape of water and earth. The land of dikes and rice fields! The intense greens and golds of midday were softened in the mysterious mists of dawn, a mystery of the mingling of land and water not yet entirely dissipated by the brutal air warfare. And everywhere, pocking the landscape, the pothole shelters and craters of the bombs. The dates of bombings can be

97

reckoned by the rate at which these holes are filled with water. For this, like a kind of pre-Baroque Venice, is a land of canals and water, in which solid portions of land mean an immense victory—although a victory of another kind than the Doges would have known.

We arrived about seven o'clock, to be met by the head of the cooperative and his female assistant. Various other smiling dignitaries and workers also approached to shake our hands and welcome us, our breaths chill on the air in that pre-morning darkness when the rising of dawn seems unlikely and even miraculous.

How lovely that morning was, and how grateful my memory is for it! We had traveled the bitter cold along dark roads, passing the multitudes of people, the camouflaged convoys that bumped along the narrow road like elephants in procession. We arrived like visitors of the Emperor, between the flooded fields, at the edge of a long dike that led through a noble perspective, to the reflected image of a large villa in the French style. We exchanged greetings and entered and were seated by smiling invitation. The windows were still closed and the lanterns lit; then, within fifteen minutes of our arrival, after servings of the first inevitable cups of scalding tea, the shutters were thrown open. The dawn flooded in upon us like the first assailed day of creation.

(What follows is the substance of the welcoming talk given us by two men; first, the director of the whole cooperative; then, the director of this village, The Red Phoenix, one of five comprising the cooperative).

Said: We grow here two crops of rice, sometimes three per year. In accord with the needs of our country and the hopes of our beloved leader, Ho Chi Minh, we try to produce five tons of rice per hectare. We are privileged at present to welcome you to one of the most advanced farming areas of our district and of our country. There are over nine hundred families in our cooperative, comprising some five thousand people. This is to be considered an average-size cooperative.

Shortly before his talk began, two women came in and were introduced as vice-director and chairman of the women's committee of the cooperative. It was obvious that the women's place in the whole farming picture was quite prominent. It was also clear that they wished to underscore the fact by the rather dramatic entrance of these women. Then we heard from the women a gentle and modest explanation of their triple role: a place "in the home, in the cooperative, and in the social works of the cooperative." We were told that Madame Vice-Director and five others in this village were following university courses by mail. In this way they furthered their skills as far as the cooperative was concerned, and readied themselves for a larger share in the responsibilities of their country.

Breakfast followed, as the dawn came up. We were invited to cleanse our hands in a water bowl at the door and to stretch our nearly frozen limbs, to rejoice our hearts with the changes of light so rapidly flooding the fields and buildings about us. I noted the intricate roof carvings of a much older building next door; it must have preceded the French occupation, I judged, for it bore a series of lovely, intricate bird and fish carvings upon the peak of the roof and along the lower edges where the roof met its corners. It was a kind of Buddhist intervention between sky and air. And badly broken, like the bones of a gull or fish that one discovers on the beach.

In answer to my questions about the animal motifs along

the roof, they confirmed my suspicion that the carvings preceded the French occupation; the handwork was included by the French in newer buildings when the farm commune was first established as a colonial project.

The breakfast that followed was truly monumental. It began with bowls of the delicious glutinous rice, which we had first tasted in Laos. Then there were courses of steaming chicken, and roast beef and pork, all with gravies, and intermingled with servings of delicious Vietnamese tea.

(For the speech that followed the breakfast I quote from my notes.) Said: The more the air war is escalated, the more food we have produced. Indeed, a Belgian visitor recently remarked, "In Europe, a comparable bombing would have brought the food situation to paralysis within the week."

Continued: In the district, the products are rice, maize, sweet potatoes, and berries. (1) We report first of all on the rice production. In 1966, due to the bombings, irrigation was seriously damaged and produced only 5.4 tons per hectare. But in '67 this has advanced to 5.8 tons. Maize is at 2.4 tons. Potatoes: some in our district have produced up to 7.6 tons last year. (2) We have considerably rebuilt the damaged irrigation systems. (3) We have also rearranged the rice fields and the neighboring irrigation. The fields used to be of haphazard size, both big and small. Now, as you shall see (and as we did see), all the fields are regular and square, and the water is conserved much more efficiently. There is a great national project afoot "to liberate the shoulders." This refers to the massive work of straightening of miles of dikes between the fields, thus readjusting the fields themselves for better water distribution. But most of all, the project has to do with ensuring that carts could be driven along the dikes, and the shoulders of the peasants liberated from the enslaving burdens of buckets of manure, or buckets of rice harvest, or anything in between. They now announced (and the announcement was later vindicated when we saw dikes stretching to the horizon like a Texas road) the end of that form of slavery.

Continued: Now we are about to begin a kind of modest small-scale mechanization.

(There followed yet another incantatory summoning of the presence of Ho.) We are building a village which is a strong reinforcement to our fighting heroes. We are confident because our state has taken the correct line. (It was a kind of liturgy, a religious chant which we had already grown used to.)

We went outside for photos after our heroic breakfast. And there we saw stretching ahead of us the innumerable individual bomb shelters. They ran from the irrigation ponds, filled with water lilies, on into the rice fields, beyond and beyond, circular in shape, about four or four and a half feet deep. They differed from the single-person shelters we had seen in town in not yet being lined with concrete piping. At the edge of each shelter lay, instead of concrete manhole cover forms, a lid of heavy woven bamboo.

In order to educate the peasants in the effectiveness of the one-person shelter, we were told how an instructor from the city would dig a hole in the ground with a single finger, up to the first or second joint. Then he would stand above, take a handful of maize or rice, and pour the grains out through his hand as though he were trying to hit the little hole. It would almost never be struck. In such a way he could show them that a direct bombing hit would practically never occur if a man took refuge in such a shelter.

We were told that the bombers were in the area. Since about eight o'clock they had been approaching the village.

Sure enough, about 8:17, with the sun firmly in the sky and the chill air receding, we were escorted to the shelters. I remember, and the memory will invade my dreams for a long time, the sounds of wooden clogs on the brick walks, as the villagers made for the shelters. At 8:17 we were underground and could hear the distant boom! boom! as the big bombs struck in the sodden fields around.

Alert

The sirens are loosed on Hanoi
a Stalingrad
ringed round, rained upon, fired—

the air force calls
like a whistle of game cocks at dawn
like a song of songs
like the embassy eagle
on whom the sun never sets
the celibate, the almost
        (for self will
        for lack of an equal
        killer or climber)

extinct of its kind.

There seemed to be no proximate danger and we emerged after about fifteen minutes.

I remember also, with a visual memory which approaches the sharpness of the sound of the bombs themselves, the slogans on the walls, the colored cartoons, the lettering carefully done by young people. The cartoons especially detained us. We saw there, pictured with accuracy and savagery beyond praise, the features of our leaders, Johnson, McNamara, Rusk, Westmoreland. It was particularly delicious to see their skill in caricaturing a general. We were used, of course, at home, to such visual sword play against political leaders. But somehow Westmoreland had always escaped the blade. Now there he was: jutting jaw, eyes aloft, breathing in air purer than that of mere mortals, an Adonis on guard, ensuring the legitimacy of both death and life.

We saw also quick, nervously sketched maps of North and South Vietnam, recording the attacks on southern cities in the previous two weeks, as well as the new air strikes against the North. And we were struck with the right use of such space as was available to chart the rise and fall of the fever of the war. One had the feeling that there were areas of communication and feeling open to these people that the sophisticated West might indeed come to envy.

The little square of the village was paved with red tiled brick. There was a loudspeaker in front of the cultural center, a modest two- or three-room structure used for village meetings and celebrations. It was built in the round, and we were told it had been erected by the Young Pioneers.

We put the question to the villagers that we had so often put as a kind of tease to the intellectuals, the army people, and our hosts. What difference do you notice in your lives here since the revolution? The answer was in one sense a cliché, in another sense too laden with dignity and convic-

tion to be anything but a fresh response. "The main difference is that we now have enough to eat."

We were told in the course of the day how North Vietnam, formerly considered a rather barren agricultural
country, was not exporting rice to Indonesia and Hong
Kong. This, while South Vietnam, formerly considered the
fecund rice basket of the East, had begun importing rice
since the massive defoliation and uprooting of village
peasants.

More incidental news: In 1965, in twenty-eight days, our
village succeeded in rearranging the dikes and straightening them. The villagers also cleared twenty-three kilometers of dike roads and set up irrigation systems, and
planted some 23,000 pine trees to guard the rice plants
from the typhoons. They had also planted thousands of
soan trees; the leaves are used for fertilizer, and the wood
is also very important for the building of new houses.

We saw a field in which a sign had been set up; they
translated it as follows: "This field is an experimental area
which is now producing, by the scientific use of fertilizer
and new planting methods, nine tons of rice per hectare."

We came out through the fields as the mists lifted, and
the full beauty of green and water spread outward before
our eyes, straight and true at the angles. We were, for the
first time in our tortured journey, in the heart of the gentle
East. It was the first Asian scene that could correspond
with our expectations, drawn from the history of China
and, deprived Westerners as we were, from the *National
Geographic Magazine*.

Yet it was war. And again all our expectations of scenic
perfection were shattered. For in the fields we came upon
a large, built-up crater of mud, with a wall about five feet
high; it housed, as we peered over the edge, a militia crew

of women. And there in the midst, like an iron spider in its lair, a three-legged antiaircraft gun.

We learned: November 1967 had marked the first downing of an American F-105 plane with these guns and emplacements. They are 20.7 mm. guns. All the young men and woman of the village know how to use this machine. Our village was last bombed on April 28 of the past year, with explosive bombs. In the autumn, in October, the Americans first used CBU bombs. In that month a boy was killed, and two boys cutting rice in the fields were wounded— all by pellets.

We passed along the dike road small groups, three or four in size, of leather-faced, smiling older folk of the village. It was explained to us that these men and women took care of the trees, hoeing the earth gently around the edges of the dike to allow for more favorable growth. It struck us again how all age groups were contributing, willingly and with a kind of contentment, to the improvement of the argicultural scene.

Before leaving the antiaircraft emplacement we were introduced to Miss Cam, the commander of the antiaircraft unit. She and an auxiliary presented Zinn and me with wide-brimmed antipellet hats, developed in the course of the air war. We took them with us, all the way home. Miss Cam, like most of the women we met who share heavy and even literally killing responsibility, seemed to us demure and gentle. She assumed a kind of formidable air only as she sat on the turnstile and demonstrated for us how she shouldered the harness controlling this air-bound iron bronco.

We stopped to visit a family that had "made it." It was explained that in the village communes there were four stages of peasant development. In the first stage the family dwelling was made of straw. In the second stage, wood was used; in the third, the walls were of brick, though the straw roof was retained. And finally the family graduated to brick walls and a tile roof. We were told that the houses we were approaching had belonged to one of the poorest of the village families only five years ago. Now they were dwelling in a new, one-room house. There was handcarving of a delicious quality above the roof beams. When I asked about the inscription, it was translated: "For a long life." Of the three sons, one was our host at the tea ceremony; two others were in the army; the sister was in the youth brigade. On the wall were documents testifying to the excellence of the work of the sons and father. There was a cartoon on the wall outside; it showed a cowboy Johnson riding a mount, with the face of Marshal Ky.

(What follows is taken at more or less random speed from the notes I made at the conclusion of the day.)

The organization of everything we have seen seems to respond to the consciousness of the people. And this integrity makes up, as far as one can judge, for the lack of machinery and technological savvy.

The electricity, as we saw on a few poles between which wires were strung, comes from Hanoi. But its use is strictly controlled, for the grinding of grain and for the use of the village loudspeakers.

Before 1954 about thirty landlords controlled all the families of the commune, together with their land. Less than 30 percent of the land of these villages was privately owned before that time. Some of the former landholders and exploiters were now members of the cooperative; the rest in accord with their own desires, were still farming on their own. The chairman of the farming commune, who had a good, weathered intelligent face, told us that he formerly had been a renting peasant. Some 70 percent of his crops had gone to the landlord.

Reported: Before the revolution there had been practically no irrigation. If, according to the cycle of rain and drought, water was available, the people prospered; but if there was a drought the people suffered intensely.

Much of the land we saw, they told us, had formerly been a wasteland. It had been perennially waterlogged or drought-stricken. But now electricity helped in certain areas; for instance in this village it carried the water seven kilometers from the Red River. We were told of a saying of the peasants: "In the days of the French, the summer crop was rotten and the winter crop was logged with water."

We visited a kindergarten, and were delighted to see the healthy, skittish children ranged along the wall, ready to sing for us. We were handed a bag of sweets to distribute to the children. So we did, feeling slightly uncomfortable in our Western skins.

We were told in the course of this day, again and again, how hard it was to describe the depth of change in the lives of the people since the revolution. "But we have a saying, 'as the sky is far from the earth, so is our life from life before our revolution.'"

The North Vietnamese referred to "political education in the village." We had heard the same term used with regard to the fliers, with what we took to be an ominous overtone. Here it seemed simply to mean the arrival of villagers at a state of consciousness corresponding to the realities of their societal life. Which is to say, they were in no sense called to become something other than peasants. But they were asked to assume a more conscious place in a structure whose outlines had heretofore been totally obscure. So, for example, at present in these villages, no one is illiterate.

Books and documents can be studied. "This is a great contrast. Since before 1954, 60 percent of our people were illiterate. And in 1945, some 95 percent were illiterate."

We asked about the governing structure of the village.

The whole village meets, we were told, once a month. The twenty-one members of the administrative committee are elected by this monthly meeting.

We heard the structure described for us. There is a chairman, four vice-chairmen. One of these latter is in charge of planning and technique; the other three are in charge of the cattle, fish, and financial enterprises. Sixteen of the members are in charge of teams of production.

And was the economy of the commune entirely state owned?

Responded: The state economy, as it affects us, is a mixed one. Certain sectors are under state control, certain others under our direct control. For instance, the state controls and distributes all the rice production, paying us according to an agreed just price. All other production is in control of the cooperative itself. Therefore the governing committee looks to two main objectives with regard to our local situation: (1) a better diet for our own peasants and (2) experimentation with better breeding and farming methods.

We were told; 90 percent of the produce of the commune is sold to the state. Ten percent can be sold as individuals wish.

Incidental: We had a marvelous celebratory banquet at noon. As was the case at breakfast, all the food had been raised on the cooperative. Among the dishes (and it must be admitted that my memory is inhibited by the local alcoholic offerings) I remember dishes of roast pork, of Vietnamese carp, of various salads, of beans, of tea. And always of course the indispensable staple was pressed upon us, the local "sticky" glutinous rice.

Conversation went this way and that during the meal. I remember asking about the Vietnamese sense of the family, how this ancient structure, whose vitality had so often been shown to us in the course of the week, was preserved under the Marxist system.

We were given a parable in response. Or was it a parable? In any case we were told how each member of a family, as he assumes leadership by marriage or parenthood, records the history of his own branch, rolls it in a rice-paper scroll, and inserts it in a bamboo tube, where it is pushed up under the eaves between the thatch and the rooftree. In this way it pushes backward the older tubes, which have accumulated in the same place, or have been transported there.

We walked the village streets after dinner, with the villagers following us, some of them daring to come close enough to meet or respond or actually shake our hands. We saw the village school, dispersed for the duration. We came eventually to the dispensary and saw it empty. But as we peered through the windows we could see the delivery room, stark as a carpenter shop; instead of a workbench, the delivery table of boards, with a solid trunk the width of a human frame, and two planks ending in vertical wooden fittings against which the woman in labor could brace herself for the period of delivery.

Chance knowledge, learned of later: There had been a young medical doctor accompanying us with a first-aid kit during this day. He had ridden in my car; I took him for granted—after a while one takes a new face very much in stride. It was only told to us later who he was. He was a doctor who had come with us in case there were a bomb-

ing that day and we were harmed. Meantime, he was
mounting his bicycle to go off. I pursued him and made
sure he was thanked, at least through a translator. It was
another experience of anonymous kindness during this long
week of courtesy and revelation.

(I am quoting word for word the shaky notes taken on
the eve of our trip to the village.)

Evidently something extraordinary is happening to me,
which I am not in a position to analyze very thoroughly
now. But a great gift, granted to few Americans, is in my
hands. I am so strangely and so immediately at home in
this new world, where myths are being shattered by the
immediate experience of suffering and survival. If I have
hard words for American audiences on my return it can
be only because I have seen an aspect of the truth which
is hidden from the vast majority. For the man of faith
such an experience induces reflection on what God may
mean by granting this trip. I do not as yet know what
its import is but I shortly will. Possibly, all these days will
mean nothing spectacular—simply the taking up of the work
of peace with more will and courage. Possibly, too, a wider
hearing consequent upon the changes which the Tet dis-
aster will have worked at home. But more suffering also.
To have seen the truth has its price attached.

Of course the stain of "propaganda" will be attached to
much of what I will have to say. This is the inevitable
poisoning of a beautiful thing. But why care? The fanatics
on both sides will be unable to bear with the news of the
life and death of human beings. Unable also to bear with
acts of independence and compassion on behalf of the victims.

I had been asking for several days to meet with the
Catholic community. And this for two reasons; obviously

this was my community and I would be derelict in not finding how things fared with it. Then, it would be a natural and constant question at home, as I could sense, to inquire how things were going with the Catholics in North Vietnam. For this reason we were particularly delighted to learn that on Wednesday evening we were to meet with two lay members of the Vietnamese Committee for Patriotic Catholics.

Our hosts were two middle-aged men, distinguished in mien and manner; a lawyer, Mr. Louis Nguyen Thanh Vinh, and a Mr. Joseph Nguyen Van Dong. They were standing members of the committee, which I suppose marks them as men of some distinction in their professions and in the committee itself.

They apologized, by way of beginning, for the absence of any priests. They explained that they bore the best wishes of their clerical leadership, but that the priests were very busy. During the week they dispersed to the countryside to be with the people. Our hosts said, "We sent a message, when we learned you were in the city, to Father Pierre Buxuan Ky, the chairman of our committee. He sent his regrets but asked us to transmit his regards and to take up any questions which you might wish to place."

We had just begun our meeting with the Catholics when the courtesies were interrupted by the (usual) air-raid warning. We were invited to enter the shelters. We tended, I think by this time, to take the whole matter rather lightly; but our hosts did not. They made sure that we two were escorted to the deepest end of the shelter, farthest removed from the entrance ways. Where I sat, at the far end of the concrete bunker, a tubular air vent, about six inches in diameter, broke through the roof, allowing just enough light to come upon pen and paper, and under a patch of sky, reduced and remote, to take the following scrawl of notes:

We had just begun our meeting, Wednesday at 3:30, when the air-raid alert sounded. We are now undergoing the second wave of the nearest attack so far during our visit. One even wonders if he will come out. And what of the prisoners who are under threat of "no release"? Mr. Johnson, we taste here the bitter end of that rhetoric, "We attack only mortar and steel." We are indeed not made of mortar and steel, and we are among the people, and it is the people who die.

(A dog came into the shelter with us and I thought of Cornell and ecology and the destruction of nature's gentle and precarious balance by the savages of the West.)

The people laugh and joke in the shelter. It is we who are sobered and thoughtful and sad. We bear the stigma that also pollutes the skies.

It is a bit like Selma—we are safe only among the victims. A law of history? Who was ever safe among executioners?

Two squadrons have come and gone, one high and one low.

Bombardment

Like those who go aground
willfully, knowing that man's
absurd estate can but be bettered
in the battering hands of the gods—
yet mourning traitorously the sun and moon
and one other face, and heat of hearth—

went under
like a blown match. The gases flare on the world's combustible
flesh.

4:30 P.M., all clear, and we ascend.

All in all, a little like being in a barrel, traversing the rapids. It was extremely difficult for us, who were undergoing this technological adventure for the first time in our lives, to judge how near the bombs were falling. They seemed literally to be falling on our heads. But we learned later that they fell in the suburbs, and that three American planes (two according to American count) had been downed.

I cannot remember often being angered in recent years. But I was deeply angered that afternoon. A realization smote me in the course of the bombing: the image of the room in which we had first met with the prisoners. And the solemn statement of the officer that no prisoners would be released if Hanoi were bombed by the Americans during these days. Was not a particular malice added to injury

when, to the "usual" bombings, was added the circum-
stance of our presence, the last-minute arrangements pro-
ceeding on behalf of the American airmen? But as we
learned that afternoon under fire, and as we were to learn
again in the face-to-face encounter with the American ambassador to Laos, there is a particular cynicism at work in
the high command of the war. Not only the enemy is ground
under, but regard for those who might be considered "our
own," is nearly obliterated. We are giving day by day a new
twist to that knife in man's vitals known as "total war."

Modern war, waged according to our rules, can be considered total because it ropes into its circle of fire all those
who lie within its eye—whether they wear the skin of ad-
versary or of a captive American. And that is very nearly
the long and short of it.

We dusted off our souls, climbed up, took a deep breath,
and sat down again with our two Catholic friends.

We asked them to explain in more detail the work and
makeup of their committee.

Answered: There are more than fifty priests and laymen
members. Most of them are priests, the rest are eminent
laymen. The committee itself is the national Catholic organization of all Christians in North Vietnam. It carries
out extensive social work, and encourages Catholic participation in public life.

(We found the definition vague enough, but were not
surprised. It seemed to follow the usual organizational pattern of the so-called mass movements, and the strong
Marxist tendency I had known of in East Europe, aimed at
enlisting all segments of the population in the national
effort.

Still, many questions remained unanswered in the course
of the afternoon. Were there any Catholics, priests or lay-

men, who were not engaged in this great effort of war and
unification? What would happen to religious resisters
against the war? What would happen to them within the
church as well as within the state? I thought, with particular irony, that in my own communion at home, resisters to
the war had not fared very well; witness my own travail in
South America, and the treatment accorded my brother
Philip since the pouring of blood incident in Baltimore.)

Would the gentleman comment on the history of northern Catholics since the end of French occupation?

Answered: Since peace was declared in 1954, North
Vietnam has been liberated and the South remains occupied. The North Vietnamese Catholics, from that date,
have stood with their people in the fight for freedom. Especially since the intensifying of the air war, Catholics have
been ever more active.

To begin, we will point out briefly the spiritual and
temporal losses of the Catholic community. It must be un-
derscored that these losses go far beyond the destruction of
property; it is in fact nearly impossible for Catholics of the
United States to understand the extent of our sufferings.
Up to 1954 the French had destroyed more than two hundred of our churches. These, with the help of our government, we succeeded in rebuilding. But since the air war
began the United States has bombed 320 of our churches,
and five of our ten cathedrals. To speak of only a few
examples, the Thai Binh Cathedral was bombed twice; the
cathedral of Lang Son Province was bombed three times in
one day; the hospital also was hit. We have no accurate
account of Catholic casualties of the war. But in the Phat
Dien Diocese, hundreds of Christians were killed or
wounded. As far as we know, three priests have so far been
killed in the bombing. In Ha Tinh Province, Father Nguyen

Van Ngoc was killed before the altar of the church. These are indeed great losses.

Continued: France brought us Christianity, but toward the end the Vietnamese Catholics, almost to a man, fought against the French. Many of our priests in those worst years of occupation were exiled for thirty or forty years. We consider now, as then, that our main resources are patriotism and love of peace in the evangelical spirit.

(He went on to speak of specific Catholic contributions. We found their attitudes to be parallel to those of the other groups.) In almost all Catholic areas, in the agricultural cooperatives, we have produced five tons of rice per acre. Also, in threatened villages, our young men and women have helped organize the militia. An example: In the diocese of Quang Binh, in a village called Quang Phac, the Americans bombed our people in 1965 more than five hundred times. Our four churches were destroyed. Young Catholics took up arms and fought the planes as best they could. In that year they were awarded ten decorations by the government. Up to December 1967 these young people had shot down twenty-seven planes.

Continued: At least 20 percent of our young Catholics have joined the army; in some places the percentage is as high as 70 or 80 percent.

Would the gentleman comment upon the evacuation of the Catholics into the South in 1954?

Answer: This question is of course posed to us often by foreign visitors.

This migration took place in the year 1954, when the Geneva Conference was not yet concluded. That is to say, many areas of our country were still occupied by the French troops, although their main forces had been destroyed at Dien Bien Phu. At the close of the Geneva Conference the United States realized that North Vietnam was to be freed; South Vietnam would be occupied temporarily by the French until free elections could be held. Ever since 1950 the United States had helped the French, mainly with large monetary aid. They had also worked with the French to induce a migration of Northerners into the South. Also, Cardinal Spellman arrived in Haiphong at a time when the city was still occupied by the French. The Cardinal placed pressure upon the apostolic delegate, an Irishman named Dooley. The North Vietnamese bishops were instructed to institute a migration; eight of them complied and completed the necessary arrangements. The seminaries were closed, and several hundred priests began to prepare their flocks. The story was spread about that the French occupation was ended, and the Communists were in control; so there could be no religious freedom in the North.

Continued: The migration went forward even after the agreements were signed at Geneva. The French were granted up to three hundred days to conclude their occupation of the North. They stayed in Haiphong, for instance, up to the twenty-first of July 1954.

Some of the Catholic leaders started a rumor that went like this: "Christ and the Blessed Virgin have left the North." The statues of the Savior and Mary were borne in procession to a French warship. In some areas the homes of the people were even burned, and they were forced out. This migration of course caused great suffering. Many families were separated, and remain so until this day. Up to now we can count some ten thousand Catholic families that suffered such divisions, North and South. And this is why we so long for the reunification of our country. It is only then that the reunion of our families can occur.

(Zinn and I discussed at some length, later, this version of the famous exodus from the North. We agreed that it was a substantial part of the story. But it also seemed to us that many Catholics, as well as many others of the North, could easily have been played upon by the endemic fear and mythology associated with "Godless communism." Possibly no very heavy outside influence was required in order to get the mythology into the air and bring the terror to such a point that people, especially Christian people, would see the migration as indispensable to the survival of the faith.

It was clear that in this complicated business, as in so many other exchanges during the week, we were suffering from a form of underexposure. So many questions were of substance of the matter, and yet had to be left untouched. We simply had not met enough people, enough diversity, to be able to judge whether or not other opinions actually were in the air, or if so, how influential they would be.

(Another force was at work, and I think its presence was first noticed and analyzed by Zinn. It had to do with a kind of selective process of memory, whereby unpleasant or even tragic elements in the past seemed to cast no weight or shadow upon the present. In every revolution history records brutal mass maltreatment, and even the murder of large numbers of people. This also had been part of the history of North Vietnam. But we were never able to gain any satisfactory explanation of the facts, or even, I must say, an admission that they were true. Zinn suggested that this process of filtering memories through the present had to do with the sense of the people that the revolution was really moving. People were by now decently fed and clothed and housed, and had elbow room in which to move forward into a future. So these great ameliorations made for an altered understanding of the earlier horrors. Zinn suggested that a like attitude toward their horrid history of slavery and exploitation might be in force among the American black community, if only there were some conviction that a revolution of white attitudes and black hopes were at present underway. But since there was no such hope of change it is not to be wondered that the memories of the last hundred years remain embittered; they are fed in the present fires of white racism and exclusion.)

Would the gentleman define the attitude of the general public toward Catholics?

Answer: The treatment that we receive in Vietnam is one of equality. The government has even helped us to rebuild more than two hundred churches destroyed by the French.

In 1954 many of the bishops went South, but since then the Vatican has been anxious to regularize conditions here and new bishops have been appointed. In fact it is true that under the French we, like the whole nation, were hampered in our growth. But now our chief enemy of freedom is the United States.

(At this point photos were presented to us showing a number of destroyed churches. Also, statistics were offered concerning the number of bombed buildings, some churches had been bombed while they were filled with worshipers; many churches rebuilt after the French departure had again been destroyed by the Americans. In exclusively Catholic villages large numbers had been killed in repeated bombings.)

We asked how many priests there were in the North. They said an exact number was hard to come by; there were perhaps a thousand priests and nuns.

The second gentleman said: Freedom of religion in

North Vietnam is a reality; it is guaranteed by the constitution. As a Catholic layman and lawyer who defends the rights of Catholics, I declare that this freedom of religion exists for all. In the National Assembly three priests sit among the representatives. We were offered a quotation from a priest, Father Ho Thanh Bien. He is the vice-chairman of the committee that received us today. He declared, "But for Ho Chi Minh, our President, Catholicism in North Vietnam would not be in such a flourishing state."

(They presented to me a copy of a rather large photo showing Ho Chi Minh surrounded by some sixty Vietnamese priests and nuns. He had evidently attended a kind of study session of theirs; everyone looked relaxed and joyful in his presence.)

THURSDAY, FEBRUARY 15

A visit to the Hanoi Museum of Art

Lacerated as we were by so many wounding and humiliating encounters during the week, this gentle respite of two hours was particularly healing. One felt that his heart could turn in a new direction, with new resources, almost with new might. What indeed are we to think of a people who, in the midst of a rain of death, conceive and push to fruition a museum of art? We had visited two other very different kinds of museums in the course of the week. I thought with horror and dread of our visit to the Museum of American Weaponry, and with somewhat less terror of the Museum of the Revolution. In both cases, concentrated within a little space, a history of death, inflicted, undergone, symbolized. But always death. Death as a way of life, as a method of history, as a laboratory for the concoction of the new man, as a school for his formation. Death grimacing from the primitive booby traps, death blindly and obscenely emptying his substance from the enormous shell cases of the bombs. Always and everywhere death, all week long. Death held before us, like the offerings of a macabre butcher shop, like sections of animal brains and animal entrails, for sale! for sale!; held up upon the counters of the world, before the appraising eyes of the carnivore Great Society. Death in the hospitals, death in the streets, death in the villages and rice fields. Is it to be wondered at that we were sick unto death of death itself?

The museum was a space where the living could breathe in the presence of all whose life continued in these breathing artifacts of beauty and strength and truth.

At the end of our visit a large visitor's book was brought

121

out and we were asked to sign. We were able to see at that point the impact that the museum had had upon other foreign visitors, to see there the names of many American friends, to whom the museum was an enormously important respite in a difficult time.

The Art Museum itself was a distinguished French Regency building, a former school for children of wealthy French families. After liberation it became the office of the Polish members of the International Control Commission. And finally last year it was taken over for the museum. There were three stories of galleries offering examples of three historical periods. The third floor, where we began, displayed the art of prehistoric and feudal periods of Vietnam, as well as the costumes and artifacts of the so-called ethical minorities. The second floor was given over to sculpture and medieval art, including older folk art. And the first floor, finally, to paintings and sculptures, woodcuts, and modern folk and village art. It was explained to us that because of the war many of the original works were dispersed. But we were struck with the quality and finish of the reproductions, as well as the beauty of the cabinetwork of native woods, and the austerity and dignity of the whole conception.

I was astonished and delighted to see medieval and late Buddha figures, roughly equivalent in time to our late medieval and Baroque periods in the West. I had never before seen, even in reproductions, such wild and enticing and racily humane images of Buddha. At one time he would appear as a dissolute Falstaffian, laughing to the roots of his great belly. At another, he was a kind of Job, his ribs and bones fairly creaking and nudging through his skin, his face suffused with natural wisdom and sorrow.

At such a distance, after our return, living once more

that afternoon, I kiss my hand to the people and their museum, and the people within the museum, the faces of the living and the faces of art. And I say with all my heart a great Viva! to life itself.

On Thursday evening we spent about three hours visiting two centers of so-called supplementary education. The first center was a former pharmaceutical factory; the second was a large complex whose prewar uses were unknown to us, but which now housed about seventy classes of workers from the foodstuff industries.

A remarkable achievement was underway in these places. It was no less than a massive continuing educational program, going on in the teeth of the war, of the winter cold, of the long days of exhausting labor.

I refer directly to my notes. The workers meet on Monday and Thursday evenings. Most of the workers still in the city go to these evening classes; others, now dispersed into the countryside, have their centers of study there. Anyone can join these classes at whatever age, and workers who wish to move upward and raise the level of their contribution to the society may finish courses here and apply at the university. Some, for example, who have completed courses in pharmacy, are teaching here after taking their degree at the university.

(Notes) Naturally, under war conditions, the organization of classes remains a very difficult thing. We must also keep up our production. All the teachers are medical doctors or technicians or experts who have finished at the university and are now contributing to society in this way. They are paid by the workers and the trade unions. The equipment for the schools is contributed by the factory, and the students buy their own books and personal needs.

To speak of the first factory we visited, it formerly employed about a thousand workers. Now all but one hundred are dispersed into the countryside. But this had the good effect of freeing large spaces for the holding of classes. (We saw classes being held for instance in the dining halls, the offices of management, and the large, open, factory spaces.)

Most of the rooms were lighted by one or two naked bulbs; lanterns were prepared at hand, in case the alerts sounded and the lights went out.

In one class most of the students were militia men and women; their rifles were stacked, together with their helmets, along the wall.

We visited classes whose offerings included chemistry, literature, mathematics, history, and technical courses in trade and sales.

We were told that these two centers were examples of some twenty-two schools throughout the city, which had continued their work since 1960. Those who work at their trade by day study by night and vice versa. The classes have continued in spite of the intensified bombing. Thus, for instance, if the students lost time through "alerts," they made it up at other times, so as not to lost continuity.

We learned that they studied for twelve years to finish all courses leading to the university. By way of comparison, schoolchildren study for ten years to arrive at the same point.

We were struck as always by the place accorded to women. For example, the second person in charge of all the foodstuff industry is a woman. She was petite and delightful and business-like. She was our hostess for the evening, and gave us most of the above information. She said, "Study, fighting, and production are natural companions in our country."

Interview with Phan Van Dong

We had been notified at noon that our week was to end
with an interview with the Premier of North Vietnam, and
the ceremony of the release of the prisoners. There was
every indication that we would be leaving that evening for
Vientiane and the trip home.

We were driven therefore about two kilometers across
town to a French-style villa with a large garden and a
gate guarded by a sentry. At the front steps the Premier
himself was awaiting us; he ushered us within, to a large
reception room. The room, as far as we could tell, was
without windows; the walls were covered with purple
drapes, there were bouquets of fresh flowers. At each end
of the room, a pair of double doors, made of metal. We had
the impression that the room was a kind of quasi-shelter;
or that at least it was protected against bombardment.

I have great trust in human faces; or a great lack of trust
in them, depending. I have before me, as I record this, two
photos of our meeting; one at the conference table, the
other at the doorway, as we were greeted by the Premier.
In both cases the face of this man returns to me with
particular vividness. I sense a man in whom complexity
dwells, in whom daily issues of life and death resound; a
face of great intelligence, and yet also of great reserves of
compassion. He appeared, as the conference went forward,
sensitive to the international climate, aware of every
nuance of a question, capable of carrying a subject forward, of riding with it, of bearing it further than the explicit question itself indicated. After we had jockeyed for
position verbally for a few moments, it appeared that we

could manage without a translator. The Premier spoke fluent French, and between Zinn and myself we were able to take careful and exact notes. It is upon these that I have relied in what follows.

(The usual preliminary courtesies; we sipped hot tea and slowly came toward the purpose of our visit. The following remarks opened the subjects so crucial to both sides.)

"Your visit here is of some importance, and we thank you. Our countries have been at war for some time. The war, however, will continue as long as Johnson and Rusk wish. It remains difficult for us, as well as for the Americans, to know the meaning of this war. But we ask, as a result of this visit, that you would clarify the meaning of the war for your fellow Americans. Because you are a people by and large intoxicated by the war, it is almost impossible for you to know what is really happening here in North Vietnam."

Continued: And yet, there are signs of hope! For if one compares the situation of the United States when the air war began with the public sentiment of today, one indeed marks a great change in the climate. And so one is justified in continuing to hope.

Question: President Johnson has given the impression that the San Antonio Formula is a compromise, a fairly easy basis for agreement. Could we have a few words from you on that subject?

Premier: That formula is unacceptable. It imposes conditions. Your President demands *productive* conversation. This is the language of a conqueror. He also asks for a reciprocal action on our part, but the truth remains that we are the ones who are being bombed.

Question: Our President has asked that while the talks

go on North Vietnam agree that reinforcements to the South do not increase. Would you comment?

Answer: This is a principle which we do not admit. We admit of no conditions and no hypotheses. So we repeat our demand for the *unconditional* cessation of the bombing. Then we will talk seriously of peace; as the war is a serious matter, so to us peace is a serious matter. When we make war we do it seriously; so when peace comes we will talk of that seriously, too.

Question: If talks should begin, will you comment on the role of the NLF? Their role seems to be a chief one in the South.

Answer: We have made clear our attitude to that question. If one wishes to discuss South Vietnam, the presence of the Front is obligatory. President Johnson knows this. But the fact is that he does not wish to recognize the Front. He wishes to conquer the southern part of our country. Still, one takes hope, because public opinion in your country has made some progress in understanding the role of the Front and in accepting it. We note also that some members of Congress are beginning to understand the place of the Front.

Question: In the past week [February 4–11] President Johnson has responded to the attacks on the cities in the South by a pledge to send more troops. There has also been some talk in our country of the possibility of an invasion of the North. Would you comment on this?

Answer: The political evolution in your country is your affair, as well as the affair of all friends of peace both here and across the world. The chief task is to oppose this needless and indeed hopeless escalation of the war. In this task, public opinion in your country is of the essence. The citizens must demand that your President conclude a just peace with our nation, on the basis of the Geneva Agreements. I believe that Americans will come to understand more and more that this is the only just and honorable way. As far as we are concerned, we will fight against any escalation initiated by Washington. We are ready for an increase of troops in Vietnam. And undoubtedly there will be more; they will surpass the ceiling they have set so far, that of 500,000. But this proves only that they are losing, and stand to lose more.

We also foresee the escalation of the air war against the North, against all targets—military, political, and civilian in the North. We foresee a landing of troops in the North. At first it will probably be a tactical landing, but a substantial one will follow. So also, international public opinion is beginning to talk of certain weapons which are to be tried out on this country. We must foresee all of this. This is a war, an atrocious war; and it will grow worse. Such is our attitude. We also want to tell you of our determination. From the beginning, we have had this will. We said that the war would last a long time, and developments have shown that we assessed things rightly. Now we will go forward to the end, to our victory.

Continued: We know also that such a war as this touches all people and all countries. We have called upon all men of good will throughout the world to support us; particularly we have approached the American people, to oppose a war which has done such harm not only to us but to their own nation. And the appeal has been heard. The fact that we are here today speaking of such things shows that we have made a common front. We are in combat here, and you there. We are responsible for our country, and you for yours.

Continued: We expect to win our victory here on our

battlefront. And we also wish you much success in your struggle within your own country. But that is your struggle and responsibility, a duty resting upon you.

Continued: And this is why we must continue to coordinate our efforts. We thank you with all our hearts and express our appreciation for your visit. In the future, we must strengthen the relationships begun here. We will be in touch with representatives of your movement; future meetings can take place here or in another place, such as Bratislava.

We insist that we bear no hatred toward the American people, that we bear much affection toward them. In the eighteenth century they gave the world an example of a true revolution, and we have quoted in our own constitution phrases from your Declaration of Independence. Certainly, one of the great results of our mutual struggle will be the beginning of entirely new relationships between Americans and Vietnamese on the basis of respect and peace.

The problems of America [the Premier concluded] have exploded in so many directions in your own society that it is obviously to your own interest to shorten the war, to bring it to as prompt a conclusion as possible. Because as you know, the longer the war continues, the worse your domestic problems become. So the question of the war is posed with such insistence that you must solve it.

So, too, your movement of resistance in the United States is summoned to harvest the fruits of a perservering struggle. And I have confidence in Americans.

The war, then, as far as it affects your society, is *your* affair. The affair I mean of those who are responsible for the peace movement in your country.

Let me say finally, we in Vietnam will struggle to the

end. We expect you to do the same thing in your country. Struggle is always hard; here it is hard in one way, in your country it is hard in another. Moral and physical courage are of the essence. And sometimes I am convinced that the first is the more difficult of the two.

Thus far the Premier. I think what struck us most in his manner was his willingness to take a question in hand and to explain it. That is to say, he did us the honor of facing our questions not solely as political matters, but as questions with profound human implications for the two societies at war. I think we said afterward to one another that he had dared to be a humanist in an inhuman time. And we could understand a little more clearly the mystery of the resources of this people. If its political leadership were capable of exercising power in so new a way, it was not to be wondered at that unsuspected reserves were also released at the heart of the people.

(The rest of our story is by now a part of the public record, so I shall merely summarize.)

We returned from the Premier's residence to a large hotel auditorium, where we were to take part in the official release of the three prisoners. It was pandemonium, Western style. Zinn and I and the representative of the peace movement sat together at one table with a translator. The ceremony was to be held in three stages. A member of the Vietnamese peace committee was to receive the prisoners from the military, I was to speak for the American Peace Movement in receiving the prisoners, and finally one of the prisoners was to respond.

I have the photos before me showing the three men marching in, pursued hotly by the stampeding pressmen. The airmen were dressed in neat suits of clothing, and each wore a heavy, quilted, blue cotton overcoat. (They had been measured for the clothing, and it fitted them reasonably well.) I responded to the words of one of the Vietnamese peace committee. My written remarks, which were later borne off by a newsman or someone, spoke of the undeniable evidence we had received during the week of the atrocious bombing of the North. (We omitted from our statement, by request of the North Vietnamese, any reference to a reciprocal gesture on the part of the Americans, such as a cessation of the bombing.) We acknowledged the generosity and spontaneity of the action of releasing the Americans. And we spoke of the hope that the act might set up some sort of response throughout our country and the world which would bring the end of the war nearer. (But as I have mentioned, I am quoting here from memory. I understand that radio Hanoi later quoted some passages from this statement, and they were repeated in *The New York Times.*)

I am in even greater darkness when I try to recall the response of the youngest pilot, Overly. My photo shows a youthful, burdened face at the microphone. I was on the far side of the great press of cameramen and newsmen who surrounded him like a captive animal. And so I have only an impression; that he expressed in a rather routine way his gratitude for his release and that of his fellows. It seems to me also that he said he hoped not to return to bomb the North, and that the war might be shortened. (But as I say, these are impressions rather than exact quotations.)

We returned to the hotel, and were told that we could have a rather brief evening meal together with the prisoners before our departure for the airport. It was felt (and as it turned out, this opportunity was little short of providential) that we and they would appreciate some opportunity for a discussion of our plans for the return journey.

We were led through the cavernous hotel to a rear section, where the pilots had been snatched from the jaws of the newsmen. They had showered, and looked somewhat refreshed and even elated. We sat down to a delicious supper, one of the best, as they said, in their memory. It was in the course of this meal, which went on for about thirty or forty minutes, that we weighed the pros and cons of returning home by commercial flight or by army flight. We discussed first the advantage to the pilots of going home by army jet; it came down to the fact that they could travel nonstop, arrive home about twenty-four hours earlier, and be protected from the press and television. On the other hand, there was the enormously weighty factor of the wishes of the North Vietnamese themselves. Beyond any doubt they connected the whole enterprise with the American peace movement, and the relations slowly built up over the preceding two years with Americans who had come to Hanoi. So they were understandably anxious that the trip be a symbol of independent peace action, taken at the initiative of North Vietnam and responded to by Americans who were resisting the war in their own country.

The Vietnamese thus explicitly connected the integrity of the trip, and its visibility as a peace gesture, to the fate of the American prisoners in North Vietnam, and the possibility of future releases. They had not been so explicit with us, but the pilots told us that this point had been made quite clear to them. So there was no reasonable doubt in the minds of the three airmen, as they recounted their impression to us, that the Vietnamese would connect their decision with the fate of other prisoners.

As I recall, only fifteen or twenty minutes of discussion were required before we had reached an agreement. The pilots, out of compassion and thought for their fellow prisoners, agreed that the best mode of travel home would be by commercial airline, the five of us returning together.

The decision seemed so rational that I think no one of us made a great deal of it. We had to return to the "other world" in order to discover the bitter truth; how immediately assailed a decision like this was to be, how uneducated we were in the harsh realities of the free West.

Meanwhile, there was the trip to the airport, and the trip westward. There seemed, during that last hour, no question but that the plane would arrive from Saigon and Vientiane, would be waiting for us in the darkness, in that darkness where it had deposited us so long a time before.

Could it have been only a week? If time were a question of human change and exposure, then it seemed as though we had been in Hanoi for a matter of months or years. Or perhaps the question of time was totally irrelevant; we had only to look inward and discover the miraculous change that had occurred in us, our exposure to the far end of American policy, of "carefully restricted" war, of an "unwilling conflict waged in spite of itself by a humanitarian nation."

The fact was that, quite simply and unequivocally, we had graduated from innocence. We stood at the airstrip that night, a degree of sorts in hand, at the ceremony of our Vietnam commencement. We looked down, and the ticket of our passage was a handful of flowers. Unseasonal, unexpected, fragrant, they glimmered in the darkness, the unlikely January blooms, celebration and portent. We had made it, the smiles of our teachers assured us.

My Name

If I were Pablo Neruda
or William Blake
I could bear, and be eloquent

an American name in the world
where men perish
in our two murderous hands

Alas Berrigan
you must open these hands
and see, stigmatized in their palms
the broken faces
you yearn toward

you cannot offer
being powerless as a woman
under the rain of fire—
life, the cover of your body.

Only the innocent die.
Take up, take up
the bloody map of the century.
The long trek homeward begins
into the land of unknowing.

The two-hour flight into Laos was uneventful in a way in which every ride of that sort is without issue; or rather, has at its outcome only the issue of survival.

So, too, the entrance on the scene of Ambassador Sullivan, accredited to the United States Embassy in Laos, a man at once ruthless and fascinating—that story also has been told. I should like to add a few reflections that may have the value of an eyewitness account.

My words with regard to the conduct of the ambassador may be of no great import in the larger question of the brutal progress of the war itself. Zinn and I were but one instance in a larger betrayal, whose field of action is the bodies of the Vietnamese people. And yet because a betrayal was wrought upon us, and because both the military, represented by the fliers, and ourselves, of the peace movements, were involved in an extended and even dangerous episode, it seems worthwhile to recall the event, and to reflect upon it here.

We should perhaps be grateful that the outcome was not worse than it was. Treated as we had been by American officials with minimal courtesy, and with a rather obvious effort to remain out of our way, should we not remain content with that? No. Like all resisters, we are afflicted beyond remedy with the idealism of which we read so often in our history, and in the history of political protest in the West. We have not grown used to knavery, and to that species of untruth which lies so near to the truth as to be able to wear its clothing, and to turn upon the idealist its seductive and silencing countenance.

Still, against the ambassador we had, I would think, one great advantage. Men of the truth, who constantly search their own motivation and hearts, are perhaps equipped to

deal also with that fine art of untruth known to our world
as diplomacy. And this may be a clue as to why Sullivan
found himself in a much more difficult situation than he
could have anticipated. He mounted our plane like a buc-
caneer; he was governed, I would think, by the expectation
of holding us captive to the grandeur of his office and the
charm of his personal qualities. No such thing transpired.
The five minutes he had perhaps granted himself to hold
the press at bay outside, and to win over a rather absent-
minded cleric, extended into forty and then to fifty minutes
of heated and close discussion. In that hour all of us knew
that our mettle was being tested to the utmost. The meaning and momentum of our voyage were at stake—the presence of the three released men in our midst, a prey worthy
of steel and will, the clamor of that eagle on the embassy
insignia, even now loosing its thunderbolts upon the northern nights, the promises so recently concluded by us, fliers
and men of peace, pledges so charged with implication for
the future of other men, lying so heavy upon the prisoners
of the North that their import must yet ring in our ears. All
this and more charged the stale air of the grounded craft
with drama and danger. And through it all, we could see
outside, like the eyes of a jungle night, the lights of the
television cameras, a closure of fire and anger and expectation.

What was it to be obedient, what indeed to disobey?
This may be the deepest question of the war; it played like
a wayward lightning between the fliers, the ambassador,
and ourselves on that night. It was a question as old as
aerial warfare itself, and much older. But it seemed to us
entirely and exactly fitting that the question should be
raised in a grounded aircraft, at the edge of an airstrip,

itself at the edge of that world which some men delighted in calling free—without ever questioning their own unfreedom. "I am an army career man," finally said the ranking officer, the major. "Any least indication of the will of my superiors is a command to me." It was the most ominous sentence I had yet heard in a war whose daily currency was groundless rhetoric, duplicity, body counts, and murderous ideology. Yet I must confess that the sentence also had a kind of untouchable platonic perfection. As an expression of the system from which it issued, the sentiment was virtuous beyond praise. The word was spoken. There remained only what we of the West call, with a clumsy instrumental neologism, its implementation. *Verbum caro*. We issued from the cave of Plato, where all words are indeed an emptiness, to face the world, the times, the purpose and hope outside. We issued from the cave and stood in the glare of man's eyes and of man's instruments, under judgment, under the yoke of the law.

The Pilots, Released

2.
When I think of you it is always (forgive me)
of disposable art; 50 designs drawn from the damp woodcut
of 50 States, the physiognomy of camp—

Innocence (mom), *pietas* (pop), the household gods
guarding the gates guarded by you, O proxies
for all providence   Saigon to

Rio to Congo   your chilling logic
draws blood   a blood bank   a bank bloody
check drawn on the living who thereupon
          here   there   and tomorrow by all accounts
                    are dead

3.
In the old moth-eaten plane   (one-eyed—   heroic
as a pirate carp)   the youngest pilot
lived it over and over   roped like an animal
to the water wheel   drawing up
buckets   water   blood   honey   spleen
lug and tug   104 days in solitary
loneliness   near madness   interrogations
brainwashing of that brain already
hung   high and dry as a woodcut

of himself   by himself;   *Our Boy; Spit, Polish, Literal Death.*

The fliers finished with the press, there on the oil-stained macadam, after a short general statement, delivered in the exhausted monotone of the major. Zinn and I lingered in the background. We were of no interest; the peace had lost its prey. We knew nothing of what was to come, we were desperately in need of sleep and wanted only to get apart and reflect upon the sudden explosion of all our hopes. An attaché offered us an embassy car; they wanted us off the scene, once and for all; and I refused, discourteously, as I recall. The pilots strode across the airstrip to their waiting plane. The sleek door of the jet closed upon its burden, as in a children's story the door of a mountain closes upon a piper and the village children. Farewell to the children, farewell!

The newsmen turned about, in our direction.